Basics of Video Production

Second edition

Des Lyver and Graham Swainson

Focal Press

OXFORD AUCKLAND BOSTON JOHANNESBURG MELBOURNE NEW DELHI

Focal Press
An imprint of Butterworth-Heinemann
Linacre House, Jordan Hill, Oxford OX2 8DP
225 Wildwood Avenue, Woburn, MA 01801-2041
A division of Reed Educational and Professional Publishing Ltd

A member of the Reed Elsevier plc group

First published 1995
Reprinted 1996
Second edition 1999

British Library Cataloguing in Publication Data
A catalogue record for this book is available from the British Library

Library of Congress Cataloguing in Publication Data
A catalogue record for this book is available on request
ISBN 0 240 515 609

FOR EVERY TITLE THAT WE PUBLISH, BUTTERWORTH-HEINEMANN
WILL PAY FOR BTCV TO PLANT AND CARE FOR A TREE.

Printed and bound in Great Britain by
Biddles Ltd, Guildford and King's Lynn

Contents

Introduction to the second edition

Two or three years is a long time in technology. This 'Basics of Video' series is intended to help you through the basic principles of production. The books are deliberately equipment non-specific because 'basics are basics'. We have now included references to the technology advances in the production areas and you will see that, with a good understanding of the basic principles, your transfer of learning to new ideas and equipment levels is easier than you thought!

Introduction to the first edition

This book is aimed at you if you wish to learn about video production. No knowledge, or a little knowledge, is all you need to be taken on a guided tour around a studio or location production.

It is equipment non-specific, merely dealing with the principles and processes involved in obtaining professional results in educational and training environments. You will not be a 'television expert', but if you are a student who wishes to learn about all aspects of video production, read on.

Much of what you read will be directly transferable to film courses and sound courses as the basics and principles remain the same.

It explains, in simple language, who works where and what each member of the team is responsible for. There are brief, but comprehensive, details of the types of equipment you will encounter in each area. There are hints and tips to help you choose equipment to fulfil a particular need.

You will learn the production process from conceptualization, and how to write the aims and objectives of the programme, right through to the final screening.

Our aim is to give you a rapid insight into the complex process of television, without getting bogged down in technical terms. Only where it is necessary to understanding is there any reference to technical matters.

How to use this book

Whilst you may choose to read this book from cover to cover, it is essentially designed as a 'dip-in' book. You will see that the beginning pages are concerned with the studio process, the middle with single camera and the last pages with editing. It is possible to read only the section which interests you at the moment, without reference to the other sections. It also caters for those of you who have 'been put on lighting (or any other job) today!' Each section on the crews, their roles and the equipment used is complete and needs no reference to any other part of the book.

We have both spent many years in the video industry, and now teach video production at all levels. We wrote this text as a result of being unable to find a 'starter book' which we could offer our students. Thank you for buying it. We hope you find it useful and you have as many happy years in the industry as we have had.

Acknowledgements

We would like to thank Margaret Riley at Focal Press for her totally calm approach to what seemed to us to be an impossible task in the time available. Without her support this series could never have appeared at all.

We would also like to thank all our students, past, present and future, who have not only been the 'guinea pigs' for this book but, perhaps more importantly, have taught us so much about how to explain a very complex process in a very simple way.

Christmas comes but once a year
when Santa came this year and
realized why we asked for a
secretary and some time
all he had to say was
HO! HO! HO!

1 Studio production

All television production is about the process of putting across a message, from producer, scriptwriter, advertising agency or whoever to the viewer. The viewer could be anyone from the youngest child to the oldest pensioner. Sometimes the viewing audience is made very specific. For example a corporate video might only be seen by the board of directors of a company. Sometimes it is very broad – the Christmas entertainment shows watched by tens of millions, for instance.

Similarly the message could be very specialized, or very general. What all of these different types of programmes have in common though is the tools they use and, therefore, the processes involved in production. What this book aims to do is give you an understanding of these tools and how to master the processes of using them successfully.

Two approaches

Television programmes are made from a string of moving pictures accompanied by a sequence of sounds. It is an 'audiovisual' experience. Both of these elements can convey information and emotions. The skilful producer will utilize both in ways that communicate most effectively. The picture sequence, to engage the viewer's interest and attention, must feel like the way the viewer would watch the world. When we look about us at real events our eyes are rarely still for long. As new incidents capture our interest our eyes flick rapidly to take in different views. A sound of a door opening prompts us to look up to see who is entering or leaving the room. A touch on our shoulder makes us turn and look at whoever is behind us. Although we are not aware of the movement of our eyes there is a constant updating, or refreshing of the visual scene presented to our brain.

The television equivalent of this is the changing (instantly) from one shot to another – called a cut – as the action develops. The programme director can choose not just when to make the change, but also what shot to go to next. This is different from how the viewer sees the world. In real life the viewer would decide what they wanted to look at next. In television the director decides what to show them next. This is an important piece of control that the director can use to shape the programme. The way this sequence of pictures is built governs a fundamental choice the director must make. He can either have lots of different cameras, giving simultaneous different views of the action, and achieve the variety of shots by choosing different cameras at different moments, or he can have just one camera, and each time a new view is needed stop the action, move the camera, and then restart the action.

The first choice is called 'multi-camera' or 'studio' production, the second 'portable single camera' or 'location' production. Each has its own advantages and disadvantages. Many programmes these days use a mixture of both techniques.

In studio

'Standby studio, Standby floor, Roll VT, 30 second countdown please.'

A studio production is about to start, but what does all this mean? Who is involved? What do they all do? How?

All TV productions involve teamwork, people who are working together to help each other to get the very best results from their particular area of expertise. The whole is a culmination of many hours of planning and preparation which will turn the original idea into a successful programme. Television is an audiovisual experience, both sound and pictures are involved and must complement each other perfectly. If this is to work properly the programme will be the pinnacle of a large base of preparation. A good estimate is that an hour of recorded programme will involve several weeks in the planning stage and then between one and two days preparation and shooting in the studio. The end result should be so good that the viewer has no idea about all this work at all. The viewer thinks it just happened. Any lack of planning and preparation will show in the result which will be, at best poor, or at worst unwatchable.

With so much happening, and so many complex processes involved, there are obviously many people contributing to the programme's success.

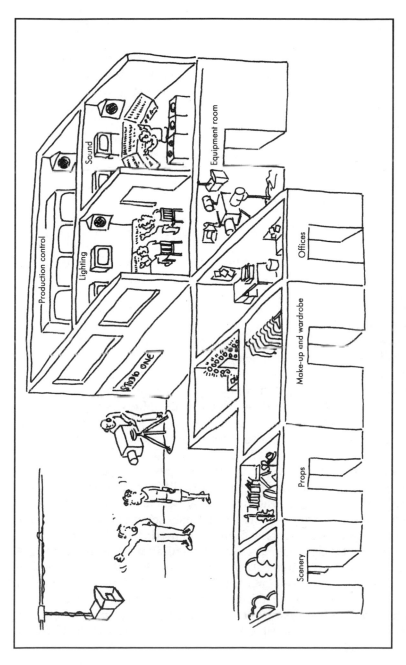

Production control

Sound

Lighting

Equipment room

Offices

Make-up and wardrobe

Props

Scenery

STUDIO ONE

Figure 1.1 Exploded view of studio as a whole showing floor area and gallery area

They are organized in teams, each with its own specialism. If you look at the credits of a television programme you will see a list of these teams. Apart from the director and scriptwriters there will be credits for lighting, sound, wardrobe, props, cameras, editors, floor managers and vision. We will look at the roles of these teams, and see how they contribute to the programme, in greater depth later. The first thing to do is find out where all these teams work.

A typical studio will consist of several areas, normally on two levels. The diagrams will help you to see how it all fits together.

The floor area

The bottom level is the studio floor. This is where all the action takes place. This floor area should be as large as is needed to accommodate the types of performance expected, but certainly needs to be no less than five metres by three metres. It should be as high as possible because the lights will need to be hung from the ceiling area.

The surfaces should be acoustically treated to optimize the sound quality. Ideally the studio should be acoustically 'dead', with no reverberation at all. Reverberation (or echo) can always be added later, but it is impossible to take it out if the recording doesn't call for it.

The floor area should be totally smooth and level to allow the cameras to move around quietly and without jerky movements. Around the outside of the acting area there should be a clearly marked fire lane, this is a safety area which gives direct access to the fire exits and must not be obstructed. The acting area itself is where all the sets and staging are erected.

Above the whole area will be the lighting grid. This consists of strong barrels or bars from which the special lights are suspended. Although some lights may be at ground level or fitted to stands at floor level the majority of the light (like the sun) comes from above. Around the walls are wall boxes. Some of these boxes will supply power to the various pieces of studio equipment, others will allow connection of the microphones, monitors, lights, cameras and crew communication to other areas. The studio cameras are mounted onto movable pedestals to allow them to move about the floor area freely and will be connected to the wall boxes so that their pictures can be taken to the control area. A studio needs a minimum of two cameras, but three or four are preferred to offer as many different shots as possible without the need for too much movement of the cameras.

A range of microphones needs to be provided to look after the sound recording. These could be placed on or close to the performers by the sound team, but some may be fitted to sound booms which are movable supports similar to the camera pedestals but with microphones fitted. Often a couple of microphones are suspended from the lighting grid as 'rehearsal microphones' providing some sounds from fixed microphones allowing the actors to be heard whilst setting up is completed.

The whole area is going to get very hot, and is totally enclosed, so very powerful air conditioning must be fitted. It is essential that either this is totally silent or it can be switched off during recording, otherwise the microphones will pick up the noise and add it to the recording. Often purpose built studios have very high ceilings to allow the heat from the lanterns to float up away from the acting area. The studio floor area is under the control of the floor manager and his team.

The rooms around the studio

Close to the studio, and with access to it, will be a collection of specialist rooms like the scenery bay where all the scenery and props are stored, the technical store where the microphones and lighting equipment are stored, workshops for the manufacture and repair of scenery, rooms for the performers like wardrobe, where the costumes can be stored, make-up and dressing rooms. Ideally there should be toilets and a canteen facility within the studio area – people will be in studio all day! How many specialist rooms there are will depend on the size of production that a particular studio normally handles.

The gallery area

Studios vary in layout for the specialist areas. Normally there is a gallery area above the stage area and looking out over it via a large double glazed window. Sometimes this area is at ground level, but it will always allow the stage area to be seen. This is the Control Room. Working in here will be the director, the director's assistants and PA, the vision engineer and vision mixer. There may be a technical director, lighting director and sound supervisor.

Here there will be a collection of monitors, one for each camera and one for each of the other sources to be used in the programme such as video

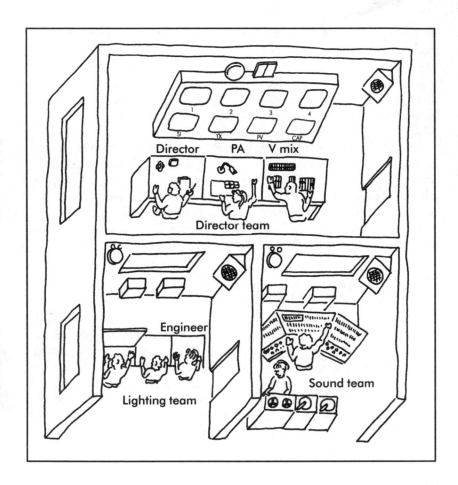

Figure 1.2   Breakdown of gallery area into team areas

tape inserts, slides, films and graphics. There will also be monitors to allow a source to be previewed before it is finally taken to an output monitor which shows the picture that is being recorded.

The source monitors are normally black and white, primarily for reasons of expense but also because elements of a picture are more easily judged and adjusted in black and white. The preview and output monitors will be colour. These images can be clearly seen by all the people in the gallery. The director will have the ultimate decision as to which picture is sent to the output. The vision mixer will have a vision switcher or vision mixer to allow any selected picture to be either previewed or sent to output.

The lighting control area

In this area will be the lighting team. They will have remote control of the brightness of all the lights using a dimmer control board. They may be in the gallery area but do not need to be. It is not necessary for them to see the floor directly, but they should have a monitor to allow them to see at least the output and, preferably, a switched monitor circuit to allow them to select the output from the cameras. Both these monitors should be in colour.

The sound control area

This is the area where the sound team work. It may be in the gallery area, but not necessarily. Again, they do not need to see the floor but must have an output monitor and, preferably, a switched monitor circuit to be able to select any camera source. A sound mixing desk and any ancillary sound sources, e.g. DAT machines, open reel tape recorders and CD machines will be here. There will also be special effects units (reverberation, compressors, gates and equalizers). The sound team's job is to get the best possible sound quality from the microphones and other sources and feed it to the output for recording onto the video tape recorder.

The vision engineering area

Sometimes in the gallery area, but often in a separate area, will be the vision engineering team. From here the cameras' apertures, colour balances and black and white levels can be remotely controlled so that all the pictures look identical. With some fixed use studios (such as news studios), even the camera can be remotely controlled doing away with the camera operator altogether. Also the responsibility of the vision engineering team is the control over the picture quality output of the other sources such as video tape recorders and film projectors. Either in this area, or not very far from it, will be the racks room where all the electronic equipment needed to control the cameras, synchronization, video tape recorder outputs and anything else needed for picture quality control.

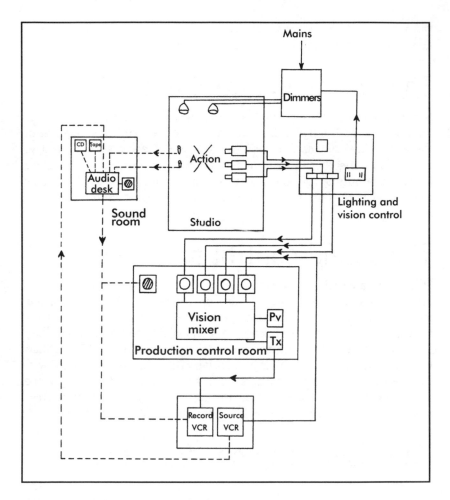

Figure 1.3   Basic interconnection of areas and teams

The machine room

In here are all the video recorders and projector equipment that will be needed during the production. A video tape operator is kept very busy lining up all the inserts ready to be used as output and checking and loading the recording machine.

Intercom systems

With all these people involved, all working in different areas, there is an obvious need for proper communication to allow them to talk to each other. The main talkback system is controlled by the director. The director is the only person that needs to speak to everybody. The director's microphone allows communication with the floor manager, cameras, lighting, vision engineering, sound, machine room and anybody else connected with the actual production. Although they can normally talk back to the director, they should not do so unless specifically requested by the director. Once the setting up and rehearsals have finished the crew only need to take instruction from the director.

Individual teams, however, may also need to communicate with each other. Because of this there may be any number of separate intercom systems to allow people to work in their teams and take instructions from their team managers or the technical director.

Health and safety

Before we look at exactly what all the teams do and how they do it, we need to consider that the studio is a very large, specialist complex. Not only the people that work in it, but performers and the public are legally expected to be protected from accidents whilst in the premises. The whole area will need a fire certificate to prove that it has been inspected by the fire officers and that it is possible to evacuate everybody safely in accordance with the law. This will mean that any designated fire exit will have to be clearly marked, as will fire passages to these exits. The exits must be suitably illuminated and able to work on a battery standby system so that they will remain illuminated even if the main power is cut off.

There should be a fire alarm system to warn everybody of a fire and it should be tested regularly. It is a legal requirement that fire drills are carried out. Suitable numbers and types of fire extinguishers must be kept in all the areas. There are special types of extinguishers for different types of fire. Water-based extinguishers must not be used on anything electrical.

Apart from fire regulations there must be a clear policy for any first aid needs. There should be a suitable first aid box available and a known procedure for reporting any accident. Again industrial injuries, and particularly any injuries sustained by the public, are subject to law. Proper records must be kept regarding exactly what happened, when and how caused as well as the outcome.

Particular regard should be paid to the lights which are hanging from bars on the grid. They must be adequately secured by at least two systems. Apart from being fixed using a bracket they are normally safety-chained or wired to the grid as well. All their leads, plugs and sockets must be secure and inspected regularly. If one light takes ten amps and there are many lights on the grid, it is not difficult to imagine the amount of electricity that is available just to lighting! Lights become extremely hot so cables and fingers must be protected to prevent them burning.

The cameras, needing to be moved around the floor area, will have long trailing leads connecting them to the wall boxes. It is essential that these are neatly coiled away when not in use and properly controlled when they are being used. Anything that moves, cameras, dollies, booms, light fixings for example, must have brakes which must be applied when the equipment is parked.

Nowadays most intercom headsets work on the radio principle and do not need leads, but some still have long leads going to the wall boxes. Particularly at risk are the floor manager team who may be anywhere on the floor at any time. This team is responsible for the public and performers and it is their responsibility to make sure that they are safe. It would not do if either tripped over a floor manager's intercom lead! There are many other examples which are mainly common sense, but one golden rule is 'definitely no food or drink in any operating area'. A cup of coffee is probably the most lethal weapon in any studio.

No area is safer than any other. This is particularly true of dressing rooms, wardrobe and make-up where care must be exercised and regular checks made. It is the team manager's responsibility to ensure that the area they are responsible for is safe at all times.

2 The director's team

The very core of the production is the director and her or his team. Every programme must have a Director. Most will have a Production Assistant. Many will have a Producer. Some bigger, more complex, more expensive programmes will have an Executive Producer. What do these people do and how do their roles interlock?

In simple summary the Director is the person who makes the decisions necessary to execute a programme. The PA is the person who provides administrative, and organizational support, and who, in rehearsal and recording, provides everyone with timing and script information. The Producer is the person with overall management and legal responsibility for the programme.

The Executive Producer is the person who ensures that the necessary finance, and other resources, are available, and that the programme fits well into its series, or fulfils the requirements of its end-user. In many smaller budget programmes the roles of Executive Producer and Producer happily telescope into one person's job. For small production companies, working on small-scale programmes, these two roles are also taken on by the Director. Few productions can manage without the help of a PA. All must have a Director.

The director

The role of the Director is both one of the most satisfying and one of the most demanding roles in production. Whilst in television there is less tendency for the 'famous author' type of Director that is common in film (e.g. Hitchcock, Welles etc.) the role is nevertheless crucial. This person alone can influence directly every aspect of the programme. This person alone can, and must, make every production decision about the programme.

Only the Director is able to see the global effect of the various contributing elements of the programme (performers' actions and speeches, camera shots and positions, effect of various sound cues, types of vision mix transitions etc.) and have the authority to change and modify them to the better success of the programme.

It is the Director who instructs the crew and performers about how exactly to execute his or her vision of what the programme should look like. If the production team is like an organic body, the Director is the brain of the body, collecting, analysing and deciding on information, and then giving instructions to the 'muscles' (crew and performers) about how to be more effective. The Director doesn't operate anything, but must have an all-seeing eye, an all-hearing ear, an anticipation of everything before it happens, and the ability to make clear decisions instantly. It is less important that those decisions are 'correct' or aesthetically good than that they are positive, and happen when they are needed.

The Director must have a clear vision of how the whole programme is built. This will embrace not only the global shape and structure of the whole programme, but also the small details of execution. It is in the methodical achievement of the small details that the hardest part of the Director's work lies.

The programme

Let's go through the progress of a Director's work on a programme. In the very beginning there is an idea to be communicated and a target audience it is aimed at. This is the seed of the programme. If the programme is being made for a client they will have some idea of what is wanted. This could be very imprecise, or a detailed brief specifying every element of the programme.

The Producer, if the programme is to have one, will already have worked out the treatment of the programme before the Director is hired, but on smaller scale productions the Director will have to conceptualize the line the programme will take. The treatment is a plan of that line, specifying the scenes, or sequences of the programme, what they put across, how they are executed (i.e. what production tools are being used), and the order they will occur in. Most programmes are linear with one scene leading to another in logical order. Linear or not, the treatment is necessary to give a description of how the time blocks of the programme fit together.

Once the treatment is complete, the Director moves on to much more detailed preparation. The key to this is the storyboard. We look in more detail at all the documentation later, but put simply, the storyboard is a diagrammatic chart of all the shots in the programme, in their correct order. Working this out enables the Director to check that the sequence of shots does actually work, with no jarring, or illogical cuts. It also sets the shots against their dialogue, action, sound and possibly lighting cues, to ensure that all of them complement each other to push the programme forward, rather than conflicting.

In parallel with the development of the storyboard runs the preparation of the script. On a complex programme the Director may well have the assistance of researchers and scriptwriters to develop the script, but often they will have to do it themselves.

The scripts

The script takes two forms (not always separate documents). The dialogue script gives the words to be spoken by performers with indications of their actions. This does not need specification of shots, or other technical matters since it is primarily used for preparation of performers. The shooting script on the other hand specifies in precise detail every aspect of the programme.

To be able to develop a shooting script fully a Director needs more than the flow of the words and actions. She or he needs a mental picture of how all the production tools are to be used. For this other specialists need to become involved. The Designer will create the visual style of the programme, designing set, costumes and graphics. From much discussion between the Director and Designer will emerge floor plans and perhaps models of the set.

This enables the Director to start the process of camera planning – choosing which camera from which position will take which shots in the programme.

The preparation

By now the casting of the programme will be well under way, and the director must organize a rehearsal schedule for the performers. Early rehearsals will be away from the expensive environment of the studio. Lighting requirements will be discussed with the Lighting Director, sound with the Sound Supervisor. Costumes and props must be organized with the wardrobe and props departments. Shots will be planned with the Camera Supervisor.

All of this planning, organization and preparation could take a period of many weeks, or as little as a couple of days, but its culmination comes when the Director leads the team into the studio. Here the Director first ensures that all the set building, light rigging, and other physical preparation is working out. Then the performers' moves and actions need to be 'blocked' – or fitted into the real set. A detailed briefing of cameras, floor team, lighting, sound and vision mixer will ensure that they all understand how their contribution fits into the whole programme.

The rehearsal

The first rehearsal using all the technical apparatus – called a 'stagger through' – will have many problems which require it to stop (hence 'stagger'). The Director must clearly discern where the most serious problems lie, and decide on methodical solutions to them. A frequent trap here is to go back time and again to the beginning to try to sort it out. What happens then is that the beginning of the programme gets heavy practice whilst the end (maybe just as problematic) gets hardly any. The trick is to accept that at this stage perfection will not be possible and to move on when the large difficulties have been dealt with. Later rehearsals will refine the lesser problems away.

The next stage is to try rehearsals at full speed, ignoring minor problems, but noting them for correction at the end of the rehearsal. It is important to remember that many difficulties only become evident, and therefore can only be solved, when the programme is moving along.

The Director must be especially sensitive to the energy, and psychological state of his or her team, especially the performers. If people feel tired, or confused, anxious, or bored they will not deliver well. A good Director will inform and encourage everyone involved in their production.

The recording

Finally the Director moves towards recording. More than one take of the programme may be needed, but again the Director must be sensitive about what his or her team can deliver. The programme may have minor flaws. The question is, can they be improved on? If so then another take is appropriate. If not the Director should consider recording correction 'pickup' shots or sequences for subsequent editing in (making sure that the shots will cut together). There is no point in doing another take 'just in case' – it will only irritate and tire crew and performers, who will inevitably not deliver as well.

The production assistant

The role of the PA is one of the most important, and perhaps one of the most under valued, in the whole production team. In the past the TV industry, with sexual discrimination common, and fairly rigid hierarchies of career progression, has had predominantly female PAs who have often not achieved their full potential, and frequently had their valuable contribution unrecognized. Nowadays, with attitudes beginning to improve, and much more flexibility of employment, PAs are both male and female and can look to progression to Director or Producer later in their career.

What do they do? Well almost everything! During early preparation of a programme they will do much of the essential administration of the programme. Co-ordinating crew, booking resources, generating and distributing information such as call sheets, budget breakdowns, scripts, camera cards, are just some examples of the work of the PA. This may be considered tedious, but remember that the success of the programme rests on good preparation, and the PA is at the heart of this preparation.

The PA will also, even in the early stages, have considerable influence on the aesthetic content of the programme. Directors often use the PA as a sounding board to discuss and shape their production decisions. Often the PA will attend early briefings of designers, lighting supervisors and so on, and will not only take copious notes of the outcomes, for future use in contracts, specifications etc., but will also have suggestions to make. Very often the Director is given the freedom to take an overall creative view by the thoroughness of the PA's grasp of interlocking information. If, for example, a Director, in discussion with a designer asks about the possibility of having a split-level set with a grand staircase connecting the levels, the PA may remind her or him that the studio they are booked to use does not have a very high lighting grid, and there could be problems with sufficient headroom.

As the development of the script progresses further, the PA will become increasingly involved in detailed time planning within it. All broadcast programmes, and many non-broadcast ones, have strict time limitations placed on them. These can only be observed if the whole programme is planned with time in mind. This is a central part of the PA's role. Sometimes a PA is asked to direct inserts for the programme, particularly if these are on location.

In the studio

Once the programme moves into studio the pace increases for the PA (as for the rest of the production crew). Now he or she becomes the all-knowing source of information for everybody, but especially for the Director. All of the information gathered as the programme has been built will be readily accessible to the PA, so must be organized. Questions such as 'How long is the clip we shot at Longleat?', 'What is the phone number of our presenter's agent?', 'How many reels of tape have we ordered?', 'When is the satellite hook-up to San Francisco booked for?', 'If we shoot scene 3 this morning instead of this afternoon can we still complete on schedule?' are all plausible, if not likely, ones a PA may be called upon to answer.

Once rehearsals begin the very specific duties of the PA in the control gallery begin. He or she will be required to do two main things: provide the Director (and rest of crew) with status information, and keep check on programme timings. Status information is shorthand for information about where exactly the programme is on the script. This entails three aspects, what has happened, what is happening, and what is about to happen. The last is probably the most important. If the Director is concentrating on instructing correctly and deciding on things like shots, sound cues, vision transitions, she or he cannot look down to read a script. Probably the Director will know the script well, having prepared it, but it is very easy to get confused about what is supposed to happen next. So the PA reads the script, and warns about what is approaching. This information is relayed verbally to the Director and, via the intercom, to the rest of the crew.

A typical speech might be: 'We are on shot 23 on camera 3, VT insert from VT 2 next. Standby VT 2. Coming to VT in 10, 9, 8, 7, 6, roll VT, 3, 2, 1 zero.' Explained this means: we are currently on shot 23 (all shots in the programme are consecutively numbered, so this gives a unique reference point); 'on camera 3' tells us which camera (or other vision source) is providing the image; 'VT insert from VT 2 next' tells us the nature of the next visual and where it's coming from (in this case from video tape machine number 2); 'standby VT 2' gives warning to that machine operator to get it ready to roll, then there is a precise seconds countdown to the beginning of the video insert, including a 'roll VT' cue at five seconds.

Less frequently information about what has happened is required. If in the previous example camera 3 (on shot 23) was holding a slow zoom in during the shot, they would need to be told that that shot had finished and the programme had moved on to the video clip. The PA might say: 'We are now on shot 24, video insert from VT; camera 3 clear to move, one minute, twenty-three seconds to end of insert.' This means that camera 3 is now released to move on to their next shot, and that there is one minute twenty-three seconds left of the video to run. This kind of back counting is vital, so that the Director and all the crew are ready for the next transition before it happens, rather than being caught out by it.

Timing of programmes

Timing is crucial to all programmes – they are planned to fit a time structure. One of the most difficult things a PA needs to do is to calculate how the actual time is different from the planned timing. Inevitably, despite the most thorough rehearsal, things go awry. This need not be disastrous if the PA is on the ball.

Let's imagine, in the example above, we are on shot 24 – the video insert. Suddenly, fifteen seconds from the end of the insert, the video playback machine develops a blocked head, and the picture coming from it deteriorates. The Director rightly decides this is unacceptable, so comes back to the live presenter in studio early. Twelve seconds early to be precise. The programme must still finish at the specified time, so the PA has to find twelve seconds more of something. Perhaps, a little later, the presenter asks the guest a question which, unexpectedly, leads to a longer answer than anticipated. The longer answer means that this section takes twenty-three seconds longer than intended. Because the two timing errors are in different directions they make the whole programme eleven (twenty-three minus twelve) seconds later than it should be. The PA will be aware of exactly how much the timing has drifted from ideal and will suggest to the Director possible ways of correcting it. Perhaps in this case the end credits could be cut a little shorter to recover the eleven seconds. Such lightning time calculation is an important attribute of a successful PA. The basic tool they use is the stopwatch, and very often two, or even three, are necessary.

Logs

As if all this were not enough to ask of our long-suffering PA, they also have to keep accurate logs of everything that is recorded. Scene number, take number, duration, reasons for retakes, which tape they're recorded on, as well as basic information like title, director's name and date of recording, must be notated for every sequence.

These logs will save a great deal of time and, therefore, money at a later post-production stage. They also form an important document for the production file, which provides a complete record of exactly how the programme was made.

Later, after the frenzy of studio recording is over, the PA will collate and organize all the relevant documents of the programme into a production file. This is vitally important as a legal record of the process, and as a ready source of information about the programme for the future. Remember, a programme doesn't die when the recording stops – it may be shown many times, be re-edited, have additional sequences added, perhaps even be sold to other outlets. All of these need accurate information, held in the production file, very largely put together by the PA.

3 The sound team

The sound team will be led by the Sound Supervisor who may have a number of sound assistants. The Sound Supervisor will be responsible for the overall sound output but may be helped by a Boom Supervisor who will work with the sound team on the studio floor operating microphones fitted to the sound booms.

The sound team's job

It seems to be stating the obvious to say that the sound team's job is to get the performers' voices from the floor and mix them with any music or sound effects from sources such as CD or tape so that they can be added to the pictures and recorded onto video tape.

This is indeed the sound supervisor's job, and to do this he or she will normally work in the gallery area with a range of tape recorders, CD machines, microphones and a sound mixing desk. The problem is caused by taking it for granted that a microphone will pick up the sound we want and that mixing it with music, or sound effects, will create the effect we want.

The sound team need to work together to produce an overall sound that is not only acceptable but is also realistic, and at the same time does not interfere with, or conflict with, the picture that has been selected. To achieve acceptable results the sound team need to know how sounds behave, how microphones work, how to correct any differences in quality resulting from inadequacies in the microphones or associated equipment and how to balance the levels to produce a natural sound. Often, like the problems the lighting team have, it is not so much a question of 'what's the answer to the problem' as 'what definitely will not work and what might'. This leads the team to consider a number of possibilities, all of which may work, from which one possibility is selected more on personal experience and preference than because 'that's what the book says'.

The studio environment

The television studio is an enclosed environment. It has walls, floor and ceiling which form a shape and contain the sound. The problems start because of the way sounds behave in this enclosed space.

All sounds start from their source and move outwards, getting weaker all the time, until they come to a surface. Here they follow similar laws as light. Some of the sound will be reflected back into the studio as audible, but quieter, sounds. Some will be absorbed by the surfaces and will not be reflected back into the studio. Simply this means that the sounds will bounce around the studio, adding to the original sound, until they are either all absorbed or have become so weak, due to the total distance they have travelled, that they are no longer significant.

Unlike light, which travels at 300,000,000 metres per second, sound travels very slowly, at around 330 metres per second. This means that the reflections are easily heard as slightly quieter and slightly later sounds identical to the original. These indirect sound waves, as they are known, add to the direct, or original, sound to produce an echo. In a studio these echoes are so close together that they form part of the original sound and are known as reverberation.

Live studios

Apart from the loudness of a sound, we also need to consider its frequency. This is a measure of the pitch of a particular sound. Frequency is measured in Hertz (shortened to Hz). Very low frequency (bass) sounds have low numbers (e.g. 20 Hz to 400 Hz) whereas high frequencies (treble) have high numbers (in the thousands, e.g. 6 kHz to 15 kHz).

Not all materials reflect, or absorb, all the frequencies equally but it is true to say that very large studios, or studios with very hard surfaces, have more audible sound reflections than small studios or ones with softer surfaces. This means that more or fewer reflections will be apparent depending on the size and surfaces of the studio. This is exactly true of any enclosed environment. We can tell by listening unconsciously to this reverberation the sort of environment a person is in, a bathroom or a living room for example. If a studio has a very high level of reverberation it is known as a live studio and the sounds appear to come from a live environment similar to a bathroom. Putting a living room set into this live environment might fool the cameras but it won't fool the sound, it still sounds like a bathroom.

A live studio often makes sounds unnaturally hollow and boomy. It may be possible to control some of this effect with careful use and placement of microphones, but it will never sound quite right.

Dead studios

The opposite of a live studio is a dead studio. This has lots of absorbent material on the walls and ceiling in an attempt to deaden the sound completely. An advantage of this arrangement is that unwanted noises from the air conditioning plant and cameras moving are minimalized.

The disadvantage is that now everything sounds like a living room environment. A kitchen scene won't sound like a kitchen. Perhaps a bigger disadvantage is that everything now sounds very dead and dry, this is particularly serious when it comes to music recordings where much higher levels of reverberation than are ever required for speech are needed to make the music sound natural.

In a dead studio with less reflected sound there is a lower overall sound level, which means that microphone positioning, and choice, is even more crucial. A dead environment also affects performers, who find it can be very tiring, not only working under hot lights, but now also finding that their voices sound very dead and dry.

In practice, studio design tries to strike a happy balance between a very dead and a slightly live environment. It is always possible to add reverberation to a recording with a reverberation unit, but it is almost impossible to remove it.

Because different materials control overall reverberation in different ways, it will always be a problem that adding scenery, props or an audience to a set will change the overall reverberation level. This means that the sound team needs to learn to listen to the actual sound and alter it to sound as natural as possible.

Sound equipment

Microphones

Microphones come in a range of sizes and prices and have different directional properties and produce different sounding sounds. It is not a question of biggest, or most expensive, is best, but a question of deliberately choosing the microphone that is most suited to the job it is required to do.

All microphones do the same thing. They convert sound waves into electrical waves that can be used in mixers or recorded onto video tape recorders. Because of this changing of the form of the information (from sound to electricity), problems will occur and this will mean that some microphones are more suitable than others for a given situation. There are microphones especially designed for speech, others for music and others that are 'general purpose' and can be used with reasonable results for practically all situations.

Microphones come in a range from very small personal microphones, designed to be worn, through various types of hand-held or stand-mounted microphones to microphones designed for mounting on booms. There are specialist microphones designed to be mounted on walls or floors, microphones designed to cut down background noise and radio microphones.

Microphones employ different working principles, some need batteries, some only pick up sounds from a particular direction, some are designed for use very close to the source, others will distort and 'pop' if used too close to the sound source.

How can we make a choice? Clearly now we can't just get a microphone out of the cupboard and expect it to work perfectly.

Choosing a microphone

Often the choice of microphone comes down to the personal likes of the sound supervisor, but we can narrow the choice quite considerably by asking a couple of simple questions. The first, perhaps the most obvious, is can the microphone be seen in shot? This is crucial because the best recordings are made by gathering the strongest sound signal and amplifying it as little as possible. The strongest sound signal is closest to the source. As the sound moves away from the source it decreases in strength very rapidly and is added to by other sounds around it, most of which we don't want.

The difference between television and radio, or normal sound recordings, is that the microphone has to be placed to fit the picture. This is rarely the best place for picking up high quality sounds.

If the answer to the question is that we cannot have the microphone seen in shot (a drama for instance would be ruined by the performers walking round holding microphones), then the next question to ask is can we have the microphone in the scene? This raises the possibility of using very small microphones concealed around and within the scene, or even concealed on the performers.

If this is not possible, and it often isn't, then we have to resort to using microphones that can be held above the performers on booms or fishpoles. Being a Boom Operator is a very skilled job. There may be two or three Boom Operators in the sound team and they may come under the control of a Boom Supervisor, who works with the Sound Supervisor.

Types of microphone

All microphones can be described in terms of their working principle, directional response, sensitivity and impedance. Whole books have been written on microphones so here we will just look at the basics.

The two most common working principles in use today are the moving coil, or dynamic, microphone and the electrostatic, or capacitor, microphone. The electret microphone works on the principle of the electrostatic and can be grouped with it.

Dynamic

The dynamic microphone is so called because it works on the dynamo principle. This is a principle of physics whereby a small coil of wire moved inside a magnetic field will produce a small electrical current. This current is identical in frequency to the sound waves and is proportionately larger or smaller depending on the loudness of the sound waves. It is often called a moving coil microphone because it works by having a coil of wire that is moved by the sound. In the same way that our ears hear sounds, the sound vibrations in the air move a small diaphragm (ear drum) to which is connected a coil (bones in the ear), this produces a mechanical movement which is detected within the surrounding coil as electricity.

These microphones are very robust and will take a fair amount of abuse. They are ideal when used on booms or hand held, because they produce very little handling noise, or close to very loud sounds. Their main problem

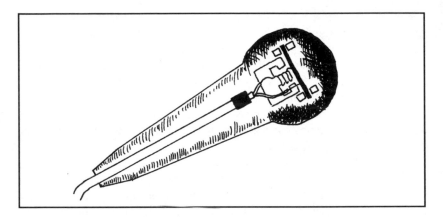

Figure 3.1   Dynamic microphone working principle

is that they do not reproduce high frequencies (treble) very well. This may be turned to advantage if the sound source is over sibilant or shrill.

Electrostatic
Electrostatic microphones work on the electronic principles of a capacitor (hence its other name). This involves a pair of flat metal plates which are quite close to, and facing, each other. If a voltage is applied across these plates nothing will happen, but if the plates are moved closer or further away, by the movement of the sound pressure waves, then the voltage will alter proportionately.

This voltage is in the region of 48 volts and must be DC (unlike the normal electrical mains voltage which is AC). It is often supplied to the microphone down the same wires as the audio using a system known as phantom power. In practice the front plate is a thin diaphragm and free to be moved by the sound vibrations, and the back plate is fixed.

The disadvantages of electrostatic microphones are that they need a special voltage and that they are very sensitive to loud, close sounds. They produce very small voltage variations and this calls for a small pre-amplifier to be fitted either inside the microphone casing or very close to it. Their advantage comes from their sensitivity to sounds which makes them ideal if the microphone has to be placed some distance from the source. They can be used on booms, but are sensitive to movement of air caused by exaggerated swinging around (producing a wind effect). Their main advantage is that their frequency response is as good as ours and, unlike the dynamic microphone, they will pick up all the sounds we can hear.

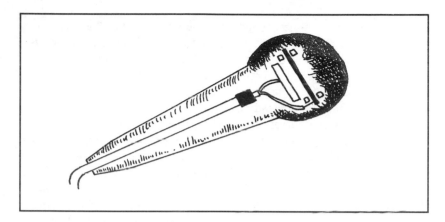

Figure 3.2   Electrostatic microphone working principle

Electret

The electret microphone uses exactly the same principle as an electrostatic microphone, but the voltage needed across the plates is replaced by a permanent electrostatic charge. This electrostatic charge can get weaker with age, causing the microphone to increase in noise level and produce weaker sounds.

Electrets do not respond to the higher frequencies (treble) as well as the true capacitor microphone, can be noisier and less sensitive, but do offer considerable value for money. The main disadvantage lies in the fact that they are prone to 'sudden death syndrome', caused by moisture or high humidity discharging the electrostatic charge, which results in the permanent total failure of the microphone.

Like electrostatic or capacitor microphones, the output is extremely small and this, again, calls for a small amplifier to be placed very close to the microphone. These amplifiers are often called 'head amplifiers' because they are fitted inside the body of the microphone casing. Because there is no external voltage supplied to electrets, a small (1.5 volt) battery needs to be fitted to supply power to the amplifier.

Radio

Radio microphones are best described using the old name of wireless microphones. Splitting the word we find that they are wire less and, if that destroys some of their magic, it makes them easier to understand.

Any microphone that is normally connected by cable to the sound desk can be fitted with a miniature radio transmitter instead. This allows the microphone signal to be transmitted, like any other radio signal, to a receiver. The receiver, normally placed very close to the sound desk, decodes the signal in the same way as any other radio broadcast and sends it to the desk as a normal audio signal.

The transmitter can be fitted inside the casing of the microphone, with a short aerial coming out of the bottom, or can be totally separate, in which case the microphone has a normal wire which is plugged into the transmitter. This is obviously preferred with personal mics, because the transmitter would make the whole microphone casing too big to be worn.

Radio microphones can, logically, have any working principle, or directional response, because they are normal microphones which merely transmit the sounds through a radio system rather than down cables.

There can be interference problems caused by other microphones on the same, or very close, frequencies, much in the same way as we experience interference with radio stations that are too close to each other. Radio microphones have quite short ranges and are not very good at transmitting through walls or steel enclosures, so care is needed with siting the receiving aerial. A good guide is to make sure that the transmitter aerial can 'see' the receiving aerial.

Legislation has recently been changed, but a licence may be needed to operate radio microphones (particularly on location). The manufacturers are the best people to explain the requirements. The need for a licence depends on use and radio frequency used.

Directional response

The choice of microphone is not limited just to the working principle, or the size, or the frequency response. An important thing to remember is that, as human beings, we can select the sounds we wish the brain to 'hear'.

Microphones respond to sound pressures in the same way as we do, but have no brain to select a particular sound from the crowd. As the sound pressures arrive at the microphone from all directions, they are turned into electricity and fed to the amplifier as if they had all come from the same place. There is no directional information to help us sort out, later, where a particular sound came from.

Manufacturers employ various techniques that can offer some directional information. By only allowing sound pressures coming from a particular direction to reach the capsule and be turned into electricity, we have a form of control over directional response.

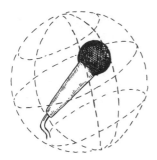

Omni-directional

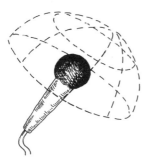

Uni-directional

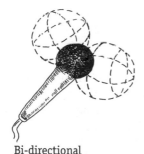

Bi-directional

Figure 3.3 Typical polar responses

This directional response is known as the polar response of a microphone. It is called polar response because, using the poles of the compass, it is possible to draw curves showing the direction(s) in which the microphone is most sensitive to picking up sound pressures.

Imagine the microphone being placed in the centre of a very large football. If any sounds coming from anywhere inside that football are picked up equally by the microphone then it is said to have an omni-directional response. It picks up sounds from in front of it, from behind it and from the sides as if they all came from the same direction. This may be very useful if you have a discussion group around a table, but not particularly useful if you want to pick up just the cymbals from a drum kit.

The first level of control is to make the microphone only pick up sounds coming from in front of it. Back to the football: only the sounds coming from the front half will be picked up. This is known as uni-directional, or cardioid (because the shape is similar to a heart).

The football example is a good one because the studio is an enclosed space (like a football), and sounds coming from behind the microphone will bounce off the front and sides of the studio and arrive at the front of the microphone (much weaker from the distance and effort of bouncing around) and be picked up as if they had come from the front. No uni-directional microphone can be a true one direction-only microphone in these circumstances, but the control is considerably better than omni-directional.

These are the two most common polar response patterns for studio microphones, although others will offer narrower responses than cardioid and are called super-cardioid or hyper-cardioid. These tend to be used more on location, but are useful in studio when it is necessary to isolate a particular sound, like the cymbals of the drum kit for instance.

A third standard pattern is bi-directional, or figure of eight. These microphones will only pick up sounds from the back and the front, but are not very sensitive to sounds arriving from the sides.

Bi-directional microphones are used as the basis of stereo recordings but are useful for 'across the table' interviews, where just one microphone can be used to pick up both people, and still offer some control of sounds coming from the sides, for example the noise from cameras or crew moving.

Stands and booms

Microphones can be attached to people or props, hand held, fitted to a microphone stand or used fitted to the end of a long rod known as a fish pole or boom.

While the other teams are busy setting up in their areas, the sound team will be making decisions about which microphones to use and how to support them. The Sound Supervisor will make the decisions and the Sound Assistants will carry them out.

The best place for a microphone is to have it fixed as close to the sound source as possible and not moved. This can sometimes be achieved by using strategically placed microphones hung from the ceiling, or fixed to the scenery, or mounted on stands to cover music videos. More normally, the microphone will have to be attached to a performer and will have to move about with the performer.

The sub-miniature 'personal' microphones need a lot of thought before just clipping them onto a performer. Most are omni-directional and, because of the absorbing effect of clothing, may actually sound more natural if they are used 'upside down' if the performer is sitting at a desk or table. This allows the reflected sounds from the table to play a greater role in the overall output.

These microphones can be concealed under clothing, but care is needed so that clothing does not rub the microphone and cause unwanted noise. Equally care must be taken with the connecting cable - a little loop in the cable, by the clip, will provide a strain relief that will help prevent rustle noises as the performer moves.

A further option involves more of the sound team, the Boom Supervisor and Boom Operators. The Boom Operator will have a long pole (often called a fish pole, because it looks like a fishing rod), on the end of which is fixed a microphone. This will be mounted in a shock-proof suspension and, although any polar response may be used, normally the cardioid response is favoured.

This whole pole is then held so that the microphone is kept just above, and just in front of, the performer's head. Care has to be taken so that the microphone and boom do not appear in shot. The Boom Supervisor will be able to talk directly to the operator and will be able to see the pictures from the cameras to check the position.

Another consideration is to make sure that moving this pole about to follow the performers does not cause shadows, from the lights, to fall anywhere in the picture area. It helps, and is normal, for the Boom Operator to hear the output from the boom through a separate intercom system. In one ear the operator normally hears the sound from the microphone and in the other ear the instructions from the Boom Supervisor. If the director wishes to speak to the Boom Operator these instructions can be relayed through the Boom Supervisor.

Booms in large studios can be mounted on dollies, which are moving platforms with controls for moving the pole backwards or forwards, as well as altering the height. These sound dollies are normally fitted with a picture monitor to help the operator judge how close the boom can be set without appearing in shot. In smaller studios, and on location, the pole should be as light as possible to let the operator hold it above the head for long periods at a time. Apart from suspending the microphone in a shock-proof clamp, the cable from the microphone should be isolated from the pole if possible. This will reduce handling and cable noise as it is moved.

Sound equipment

Source machines

Apart from the live sounds from the microphones, all programmes will have some recorded music and/or sound effects. These will be taken from a range of source machines.

Although record players are still in limited use, they can be very largely discounted. The humble cassette deck is still in use, but the quality and access time has moved it to the 'last resort' category. Most studios will still have an open reel tape recorder which has good quality and the advantage that selections of music and effects can be assembled into the right order by cutting the tape and splicing the individual pieces into the right order.

The preferred option is a digital source, of which the compact disc is a standard workhorse. It is possible to cue these up very accurately and to programme them to play the selections in the right order, assuming all the items are on the same CD!

Increasingly the DAT (Digital Audio Tape) recorder is replacing the open reel tape recorder. DAT can be used in exactly the same way as cassette or open reel recorders in that material can be recorded onto them in the right order and then indexed electronically for fast and accurate playback. As well as stereo versions there are multi-track variants.

There are also two disc-based systems in common use. One uses a standard 3.5 inch HD disc to record and play back digital audio and the other is the Mini Disc system. Both have the advantage of instant start, accurate cueing, digital quality sound and easy compilation of programme material.

Normally the music and effects that are required are on different discs, perhaps different mediums and maybe recorded from live sounds. It will help the sound team to make a special compilation of all the music and effects in the right order and of the right duration This is called a music and effects tape (or M&E for short). The M&E tape can be indexed to make finding and cueing the sounds very easy in a time pressured environment.

Mixers

Studio-based television programmes are shot time sequentially. They start at the beginning and end at the end. There is very little editing and no chance for adding or balancing sounds afterwards.

The heart of the sound system is the sound mixer, sometimes called the desk or the board. This is operated by the Sound Supervisor and consists of a box containing a number of identical channels, through which each sound is processed, from where it can either be fed to groups or the outputs direct.

Each channel should have a gain, or trim, control which is a coarse control over the incoming sound level and allows the channel to receive exactly the right level of sound.

There should be some way of controlling the tonal quality. This is called equalization or EQ for short. The EQ section of the channel may just be bass and treble controls or may offer much more subtle control.

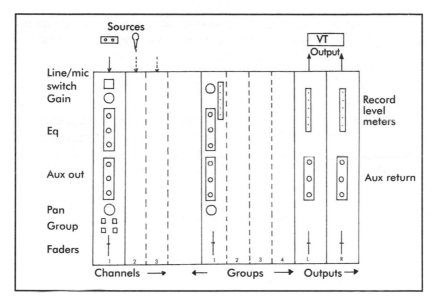

Figure 3.4   Basic mixer set-up

There should be some auxiliary outputs (Aux for short) which have several uses. The most often used are ones that allow sound from a particular channel to be cued, without being sent to the outputs. Sometimes this is on a separate button called PFL (pre-fader listen), allowing the operator to hear the sound before raising the channel fader.

Another use for the aux outputs is to send a particular channel to the effects units, like reverberation or echo, or the processing units like compressors or gates.

Reverberation or echo units are used to make the sounds from a particular channel sound as if they are in a particular environment. Adding a little reverb, for instance, will make a voice sound as if it is coming from a bathroom or large hall.

Compressors can make quieter sounds louder and louder sounds quieter. This produces a 'tighter' sound for music, or helps to compensate for performers moving further away, or closer, to a microphone.

Gates are electronic switches which will only allow sounds through when they reach a predetermined level. Useful for cutting the ambient sound from being picked up by a microphone when there is no voice, but remember that when they open they let all the sound through, including the ambient. Most mixers nowadays are stereo, so there will be a pan control to determine which track of the video recorder the channel is sent to. For mono recordings this pan control is left in the centre position.

The advantage of having groups is that a number of separate channels can be fed to one group and controlled from one fader. A classic example is when a drum kit may have ten or twelve microphones, all looking after the sounds from different bits of the whole kit. Each microphone can be sent to a separate channel and the sound adjusted for level and tonal quality. All these channels can then be fed to one group allowing the whole drum kit to be made louder or quieter with one fader whilst retaining the overall balance.

All the sounds that have been gathered together into different groups are then fed to the output faders, which control the overall level of the whole programme.

There should be provision within the mixer for something called foldback. This is a separate output which allows any sound to be fed to the studio floor. This is essential if action is cued from sound effects. For example, if the performer hears the phone ring, or a knock at the door, and responds. It must be possible to select sounds for foldback. Microphone sounds must not be fed to the floor because that would cause the microphones to 'hear' themselves, resulting in a high-pitched whistle called feedback.

4 The lighting team

Television is made up of pictures and sound. Pictures come from cameras. Cameras need light to see. Whilst on location there is often plenty of light around 'accidentally', from ambient daylight, room lights etc., in the totally controlled environment of a studio the light has to be provided for the cameras. This is the job of the lighting team.

The lighting team consists of a Lighting Director, Lighting Operator and Sparks led by a Gaffer. Often in small studios this is all done by one person. Sometimes, particularly on location video or film shoots, the role is combined with camera operator to become Lighting Camera Operator.

If we look at the full team in studio the Lighting Director is the person with overall responsibility for designing the lighting and for supervising its installation and operation. The Lighting Operator is the person who controls the lighting system during the programme. This used to be fairly straightforward, but with the increasing use of programmable mobile lights it is becoming more complex. The Sparks are the people who actually rig the lanterns and the Gaffer is their supervisor. In the past Sparks have had an unjustified reputation for being basic and perhaps insensitive souls, with no understanding of the niceties of television aesthetics, but it is worth remembering that their understanding of how to place lanterns, despite dealing with extreme heat, dangerous voltages and perilous heights, has made possible the delicately beautiful shots of many a director.

In reality, most small studios cannot sustain a large lighting team, so let's look at the processes to be covered, by one or maybe more bodies, rather than concentrate too much on the division of the roles.

As ever, one of the most important processes is that of the planning. Here it is vital that the Lighting Director understands the two different requirements of lighting so that she or he can harmonize their solutions. These two are the need for illumination so that the camera can see useful images and the need for some kind of atmospheric interpretation, so that the image conveys powerfully the required message.

What the camera needs

The need for illumination is explained very simply. The studio, being a controlled environment, starts with no light (it is in darkness) so obviously we have to give the camera some light to see by. Not so obvious is that even the best, most advanced camera does not see the world as we see it through our eyes. Our eyes are both extraordinarily sensitive and intelligent. The sensitivity means that we can see useful images even in very dark conditions. Try looking out at your garden at night, or switching the light off in your sitting room. With hardly any light you can still see enough to separate and discern things. Although there are some television cameras that can see by starlight they are very expensive and are not used for programme making, but rather for surveillance, or military purposes.

Perhaps more of a problem is not the absolute sensitivity of the cameras, but their limited range of acceptable light input. The human eye can not only see in almost total darkness, but can accommodate bright sunshine. Television cameras have a very narrow usable range from the darkest to the brightest within a scene. Certainly modern camera technology is much better than the old tube-based systems, but still the effective range of what the camera can see with is restricted.

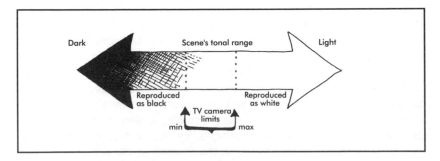

Figure 4.1   Different lighting scales

Figure 4.2   An over-exposed image will lose texture and detail in both highlights and dark areas

Cameras that can see in dark conditions would be hopelessly overloaded in bright conditions. So the nub of the problem for a Lighting Director is not just to give the camera enough light, but also not to give it too much. To be technical, the contrast ratio of the scene must be controlled. Contrast ratio is the difference between the brightest part of the scene and the darkest part. Too high a contrast ratio will lead to poor quality images. Either the bright areas will be burnt out, with no texture detail, or the dark areas will be compressed into indiscernible shadow. Sometimes you can, if you are unlucky, get both symptoms, as the electronics of the camera, detecting too bright an image, attempt to compensate by altering how the signal is processed.

Too low a contrast ratio is not a problem, except that the images may look flat and dull, but if the camera does not have enough light the electronics will lift a dark picture to an artificially bright level. Unfortunately this does not solve the problem, but merely makes what should be unseparated darkness into a muddy mid range, with little life or contrast in the image and poor pastel colours.

Cameras therefore have to be presented with just the right amount of light to give vivid images. That amount is critical, so the lighting team's most important task is to control the amount of light.

What the camera can do

The camera itself has a very crude light control device as part of its lens – the iris. This very simply allows more or less light to fall on the camera's pickup system, but it does it across the whole area of the image being unable to discriminate between dark and bright areas.

Automatic irises, while seeming very tempting to look after the tricky problem of getting the correct exposure, can be very troublesome precisely because of this lack of discrimination. As they average the brightness of the whole picture, any change to any area of the picture will trigger a change in the iris setting. This is well and good when the image is changing rapidly and our attention is elsewhere, but with the small, gentle changes which are common in production we will immediately notice the background of the shot fluctuating as the auto iris attempts to compensate for changes in overall brightness.

Really we have to avoid this, especially in the studio where everything is controllable, so the key problem for the lighting team (from a technical as opposed to an aesthetic viewpoint) is to give the cameras an even field of light at the level that they work. To the naked eye this may seem fairly flat and uninteresting, but the trick is to use the best light meter available, which is of course the camera, feeding into a monitor. As this is how the final picture will be judged the lighting team may as well ensure they are getting it right by using it as their test.

The aesthetics

The atmospheric, or aesthetic requirement of the lighting is a great deal less tangible and measurable, but luckily there are some guiding principles which will give a good starting point for the lighting team.

The most important is also the one that is easiest to overlook because it is so obvious! In a programme we are telling a story, creating a scene. We want the audience to be given an impression of a particular place, particular circumstances, that are part of that scene. So we should go back to that imagined scene to find the defining aspect of its lighting. A room lit by moonlight coming through a high window will look different from the same room lit by bright sunshine, from the same room lit by artificial lighting, from the same room on a cloudy day. All of those differences are to do with where we would expect the light to be coming from and thus how affecting the room. You could jot down a list of how you expect to see the light in each of those circumstances. This list would be the first clue as to how you could begin to build a lighting plot for the television cameras to be able to see the room as the director envisaged it. It would tell you where to place your lanterns, how to distribute the lighting, how to juxtapose light and shade.

Lighting design

This brings up the next crucial principle. When we design lighting we are not only dealing with light, but also shadow. The two together give subtle clues to the viewers about shape and texture, such that they can have a sense of the three-dimensionality of an image, even though they only see it through a two-dimensional screen. This works because the brain interprets light as being closer than dark (unless there is other visual information to contradict this). If we put darkness next to light the first thing we assume is that the dark area is slightly further away. So how we place light and dark for the camera to see will begin to give depth (and therefore texture) clues.

In the days of monochrome television this juxtaposition of light and shade was vital to give a sense of shape. Tones of similar grey become inseparable. Now, with colour, we have another piece of information. Maybe what would have looked like grey next to grey now looks like pink next to green, but it will still be given a great deal more apparent shape if there is shading to emphasize depth.

The shadow is a precise tool. From it, quite unconsciously, we pick up information about the nature and position of the light casting the shadow. For instance, look at a photo of somebody at midday, then at one of somebody in the evening. The high shadows cast by an overhead sun fall differently on the face from the longer, more horizontal shadows from a sun low in the sky. Normally we don't think about this, but accept its clues, but when we are creating a scene with light for a camera to see we must think very carefully about where our light is and what kind of shadow it is casting.

The luminaires

What are the tools of the lighting team? Obviously, at the planning stage, the Lighting Director will be working with the designer on floor plans and

Figure 4.3   Where is the light coming from? In A it comes from high above like midday sun. In B it comes from lower — perhaps evening sunshine

possibly models of the set. Later in the process he or she will develop detailed lighting plans and brightness plots. These will show where the lanterns are to be placed and how bright they should be at any moment.

Other tools fall into two main groups, the lanterns and their accessories and the control system.

The lanterns, or luminaires, are the basic building blocks of the lighting system. They come in a variety of different forms, designed to do different jobs. All of them will have some kind of light emitting unit (commonly known as a bulb, technically called a lamp, often referred to as a 'bubble'), some kind of housing to protect the lamp, some kind of optical system to ensure the light coming out is of the right kind and in the right direction and some kind of mounting or fixing arrangement. More often than not they will also have some kind of power connection.

The bulb (or lamp) size is often used as a way of defining the lantern, since it governs both how much electricity it uses and also how much light we can expect out of it. Almost all sizes are possible from the smallest (15 W) up to giants of 25 kW or more. (The W here refers to 'Watts' which is a measure of the power of the lamp. The k refers to 1000, so a 25 kW lamp will have a power rating of 25,000 watts.) Most of them work by having a wire filament which glows when electricity passes through it – much the same as an ordinary household bulb – but a significant number of television lights work to different systems (such as a controlled spark in an exotic gas inside the lamp). These latter ones will often give a much higher light output, at a specific colour (useful on location), and cannot be used on studio dimming systems, so we will pass over them for now.

The housing types are highly varied, but all serve the function of providing a safe and robust box for the lamp and the optical system. Quite often the lamps operate at high temperatures, so the housing must be able to withstand such heat safely. Sometimes they will have cooling fans incorporated within them.

The optical systems again vary widely. At the most simple they are little more than a simple reflector. The difference is governed by what type of light the lantern is intended to give out and how much, if at all, the shape and nature of its output beam is meant to be controlled.

The type of light given out is an important choice. The choice is between what is called 'hard light' or 'soft light'. 'Hard light' will give sharp focused, hard-edged shadows similar to sunshine; 'soft light' gives shadows that diffuse at their edges and have no sharp delineation, like cloudy daylight. The Lighting Director uses the two different types of light for quite distinct purposes.

Hard lights

Hard lights, with their clear shadows, form a mimic of an imagined source of natural light in the scene and their shadows give clues about where that light is coming from. A scene of bright midday sunshine would require a high overhead position for such a lantern. A similar scene later in the day might have a much lower angle for the lantern to shine from, suggesting a sun low in the sky.

The angle at which the lantern shines is a key parameter – more important than its actual position. This is because we don't look, with our cameras, at the source of light, but rather at where its shadows are cast, for instance on the face of a performer. The Lighting Director will therefore choose hard light lantern positions which give the correct angle and are convenient.

Soft lights

Soft lights are used when the Lighting Director does not want to add another set of distinct shadows. The reason for this is very simple. In real life we are used to one sun in the sky, not two or more. So a face with two or more conflicting shadow angles on it looks wrong. The Lighting Director chooses his one angle of 'sunshine', but then needs to add other non-shadow-casting light to give the camera a controlled contrast ratio in the scene. In other words the one 'sun' spotlight gives correct shape and modelling to the face, but casts shadows the camera cannot see into. They appear as dark undiscriminated areas – not acceptable. Into those shadow areas the Lighting Director points 'soft light' to lift their illumination to a level visible to the camera.

Other more specialized lanterns may have optical systems allowing, for example, projection of a shaped pattern (such as from an arched window), or the even illumination of background walls.

Mountings

The mounting, or fixing arrangement must allow the lantern to be easily pointed, so it must allow for the unit to be panned or tilted. It is useful as well for it to allow the height of the unit to be varied. Once again there is a huge variety of different types, from the simplest of tripod stands to powered hoists and systems which allow the pan, tilt, height and beam angle of lanterns to be computer controlled from a remote control desk. Needless to say a fundamental requirement of all of them is that they are safe and secure.

Many large studios have what is called a 'saturation rig'. This means that the whole of the studio's ceiling is covered with many lights, all on hoists. The Lighting Director then merely has to choose which lantern of the many available is nearest to his chosen angle. These lanterns are often double ended, so that the Lighting Director can choose whether to use the hard end, or the soft end depending on his need.

Power and dimmers

Finally the power connection to the lanterns needs some brief mention. Lanterns are the biggest users of electrical power in a studio, so it is important that this power is delivered safely to them.

Heavy gauge cable and connectors are used and the routing of the cables as they come to the lanterns must allow for expected movements and not create a hazard for people in the studio (by crossing walkways for instance). The power will usually (in studio) come from some form of dimming or control system.

The dimming system allows the lanterns in use to be set to different levels of brightness and for those levels to be smoothly changed as the programme progresses. This is done by varying the amount of electrical power applied to the lanterns. Each lantern has a numbered sign on it (or its hoist) the number being visible from the studio floor and also from the lighting control area. The numbers correspond to channel numbers on the dimming system, so that when the Lighting Operator moves the fader for channel 17, for instance, the brightness of lantern 17 will change.

There are two main parts to the dimming system. The less visible of these are the actual dimmer circuit packs. There will be one of these for every channel of the control system, usually gathered in groups of six, in cabinets containing maybe twenty-four or thirty dimmers. What each of them does is control the amount of power fed to its appropriate lantern socket, according to the level of a small low voltage control signal. Each dimmer pack, then, will have a heavy power supply coming in to it, a small control connection and an output which will go ultimately to the lantern concerned.

Often, to help flexibility, studios will have some sort of patching arrangement, whereby the output from particular dimmers can be re-routed to different lanterns when required. Once these three connections are made and the required patching set up, the dimmers operate as 'black boxes', needing no direct contact from the operators, so (because they cause some noise and require very heavy power inputs) they are often installed in separate areas away from the studio floor.

The other part of the system is the control desk. This allows the Lighting Operator to change the lanterns' brightness by operating faders and other controls. It generates the small control signals which feed back to dimmer packs, but because these are at low level the desk itself can be remote from the dimmers and it is usually placed in a vision control area, often near to the camera exposure controls. At its simplest the desk will have a single fader for each control channel, but many types of desk are available, some giving elaborate memory, auto-fade, special effects and other facilities. It is in the flexibility of what the desk can do that the creativity of the Lighting Operator can have its greatest expression. Some studios also have small portable desk units, or hand-held radio-linked controllers which allow the Lighting Director to alter levels from the studio floor whilst rigging.

The lighting operator

At the desk the Lighting Operator is primarily concerned with balance between the lanterns being used. Bearing in mind that the cameras need even light across the whole of their image, having one lantern disproportionately bright can ruin the shot. It is surprising how little a variation of a dimmer fader can alter and improve the lighting balance of the shot. Obviously there is a close relationship between camera exposure and lantern brightness – this is why the two controls are often adjacent. The Lighting Operator needs to remember that the overall brightness of the shot is best controlled by the camera vision engineer (probably using the iris), but brightness of areas within the image is only controllable by skilful use of the lighting desk.

A common fault of lighting novices is to judge the scene by their own naked eyes rather than by how the camera sees it. This is a particular trap if the director has asked for dramatic lighting. The naked eye leads the poor novice to put very bright areas adjacent to dramatically dark ones. It looks great to the eyes and would be wonderful in a theatre, but the cameras don't stand a chance. They see excessively bright areas, probably with grossly over-exposed highlights right next to deep darkness. Any attempt to correct this on the cameras' irises merely pushes the dark areas further down. The real solution is to forget looking directly at the scene but to look through the camera instead, then (strange as it may seem) put more light into the dark areas and less in the bright hot spots. It may look disappointingly flat to the floor crew but the cameras will put the drama back into it – controllably!

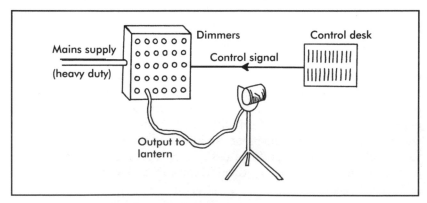

Figure 4.4   A simple schematic of a control system

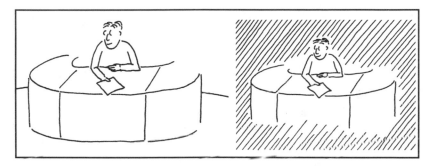

Figure 4.5   (a) Correct with camera iris (b) Correct with lighting balance

Another concern the Lighting Operator (and Lighting Director) will need to be careful about is the fact that the cameras will be adjusted to a particular reference level of lighting. This is not so much from a brightness aspect, which can be accommodated by iris adjustment, but from the point of view of colour response. The cameras (not being intelligent) have to be told what white (and black) are. These settings are directly related to the colour of the lighting on the scene. This colour varies according to variation of the dimmers, so the Lighting Operator should aim to have all of his lanterns at, or close to, a chosen optimum fader level (which will have a predictable colour temperature). Any lantern burning much brighter will look blue; any burning much darker will look red. Of course this colour variation (under careful control of the lighting desk) can be used deliberately to cool down, or warm up the coloration of the shots, but needs great finesse!

Planning

So how do all these tools get used and how does the lighting team actually operate?

The first stage is for the Lighting Director, with the director and designer, to agree what kind of lighting style is required and what if any special lighting requirements the director may have. This is the basis of his lighting plan, where he organizes the practicality of how to achieve the lighting necessary. The lighting plan will show a detailed floor plan of the studio and the set, with perhaps indication of likely camera positions. Onto this will be added symbols showing the position of the lanterns and where they are intended to shine.

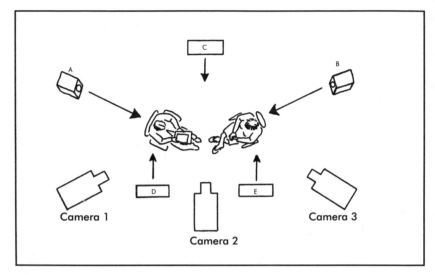

Figure 4.6   A lighting plan

Using this lighting plan as a starting point, once the production has occupation of the studio and the set is built, the Sparks will carefully adjust each of the specified lanterns to be pointing in the required direction and have any necessary colour filters, or accessories fitted to them. As this rigging may well require use of ladders and will at least occupy floor space, it must be done early before the director needs to start work on camera rehearsals.

Careful note must be taken of things like performer movement, camera movement and microphone positions to ensure that no problems occur later which would be difficult to remedy. A wise Lighting Director might also at this stage allow for possible alternative lanterns in the trickiest situations. Once they are rigged they can easily be faded up or not as needed, but if the need is only discovered later in the process and the lanterns then have to be rigged, rehearsals would have to be interrupted.

Once all the lanterns are pointing in the right direction the emphasis is on the Lighting Operator methodically programming the desk. Each individual lantern is carefully adjusted to its correct level (bearing in mind the target setting for which the cameras' colour has been set). The scenes are built up and the lanterns balanced together. If the desk allows, scenes can be stored in memories in the desk so that they can be quickly and smoothly reset. If this is not possible the Lighting Operator needs to prepare his own log to remind him how to move efficiently from scene to scene.

As soon as possible a basic level of lighting is set up so that the director can progress with camera rehearsals. This may not be the final refined balance – the Lighting Operator will continue to improve it as rehearsals progress – but the director must be enabled to look at shots. Lighting and its adjustment always seems to take all the available time, so a sense of priorities is essential in the lighting team. The top priority has to be to give the director workable lighting for shots as early as possible, then quietly and unobtrusively to improve the lighting balance!

During the programme the Lighting Operator will keep an attentive eye on the monitors showing each camera's shot and ensure that the lighting is fine tuned accordingly, before the director needs that shot! Something as simple as a performer turning their head slightly may need their key light to be brightened or dimmed slightly to keep the balance right. Throughout the process the Lighting Director is ensuring that all is as good as it can be.

The satisfaction for the lighting team is that they will have made a real contribution to possibly beautiful shots. The frustration is that their efforts, when successful, are often not noticed, but when unsuccessful will be immediately criticized by everyone!

5 The camera team

Everyone knows what a television camera operator does – they operate cameras! Behind that obvious summary of the job lies a great deal of subtle skill which is essential to the success of any programme.

The camera team consists of a number of Camera Operators, who actually work separately, getting their instructions direct from the director. In large organizations, with Camera Operators on staff, there may be a Camera Supervisor who would organize crew rotas. Sometimes (more often on location shoots) one Camera Operator would also be responsible for designing the lighting for the programme and would become a Lighting Camera Operator. Often in small studios the Camera Operators are all of equal status.

The cameras

Studio cameras are notably different from their location equivalents because they are often larger and always mounted on a movable pedestal. They will have fewer operator controls because exposure and colour balance are remotely controlled by the vision engineer. They will have a larger viewfinder, normally in colour, to allow the operator to see the shot whilst standing behind the camera and operating the movement controls. A talkback system will be incorporated allowing the operator to hear instructions from the director and, normally, the programme sound.

The reason they can be like this is that the nature of a studio production is such that the director will have a number of cameras, in different positions, from which to choose shots continuously. The studio camera does not need to be portable, but does need to be mounted in such a way that its movements are smooth and silent.

With advancing technology, and manufacturers' understanding of the needs of cost-conscious production facilities, it is now possible to buy cameras which can be configured for location or studio use. This allows much greater flexibility for smaller studios who may use a location camera, with 'extras', as one of their studio cameras. If you are considering this, remember that a Camera Control Unit is essential for it is this that will allow remote control of the electronics. There must be the ability to fit a larger viewfinder, or an output for a camera monitor, and a talkback facility which can be coupled into the studio system.

Most studio cameras will spend their life permanently installed and configured for studio use, but increasingly this 'mix and match' arrangement is being used. It is possible, and often desirable, for location cameras to be brought into the studio, connected to the studio system and then used as hand-held, highly manoeuvrable units. Music videos are an obvious example of a situation where this would be very useful.

The camera is usually mounted on what is called a pedestal. This is like a very substantial tripod, but with the ability to move easily over the studio floor, to change height easily (despite the considerable weight of the camera head), as well as the usual abilities to give smooth panning and tilting.

Above the pedestal, but below the camera, is the panning head. This allows for two movements of the camera, panning and tilting. Panning and tilting are just two of the ways that the Camera Operator can move the camera to achieve the best image.

It is a good idea to think back to how we look at the world with our eyes before we consider how the camera might move. More often than not our eyes move very rapidly (so rapidly that we are not aware of the movement) from one fixed position of looking to another. Only rarely are we aware of movement of the viewing point (our eyes), and then it is because we are following a moving subject. Similarly with the camera (which is, after all, a surrogate set of eyes for the viewer), we (as programme makers) must not be tempted to have unmotivated movement of the point of view. Much better to think of the camera as seeing movement rather than moving. Cameras which move without motivation give restless images which are difficult (if not impossible) to watch. The rapid switch to another point of view (similar to the flick of the eyes) can be achieved by the cut, and in studio that is done by the vision mixer. What we mostly want are fairly static camera positions.

Movements

Sometimes however a movement is essential – to follow a walking character for instance. The trick which Camera Operators must develop is to make all camera moves very smooth, to make them justified by movement of the subject, or to make them imperceptibly slow. Any shakiness, or jerking in the camera's movement would destroy the illusion that the viewer was looking themselves. Bearing all of these in mind then, what movements are available to the Camera Operator? It's useful, when thinking of camera moves, to think, more precisely, of movements of the lens, since it is the lens which takes in the image. This also helps to explain the jargon of camera movement instructions.

The most simple movements are the pan and the tilt. These are movements in the direction of two imaginary circles, or discs. Panning is the movement in a disc parallel to the floor, either to the left or to the right. Slightly confusingly moving the lens to the left (panning left) appears to move the image to the right. The tilt is the movement within an imaginary upright disc, so the lens moves up or down.

Change of the height of the camera head above the ground will change the angle at which the lens sees the scene. This movement is called raising or lowering the camera head (or craning up or down, or elevating or depressing the head).

Movements of the whole assembly (camera and pedestal) are tracking (moving closer to or further from the action), crabbing (moving at right angles to the line of the camera's lens) and arcing (moving in a curve around the subject).

All movements must be extremely easy, so that the Camera Operator can move the camera rapidly, but also very smoothly. This smoothness is achieved for panning and tilting by a system of damping in the panning head. So that the Camera Operator can adjust the amount of resistance to these movements there will be drag, or friction controls on the panning head. There will also be locking devices, both to allow for static shots to be easily achieved, and to provide security when the camera is not in use. Attached to the panning head there will also be two long handles to help the Camera Operator to move the camera head.

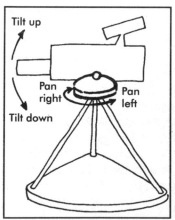

Figure 5.1(a) A panning head with movement arrows

Controls

The camera head itself is made up of three main boxes. At the front is the lens. This is the primary tool for selecting and shaping

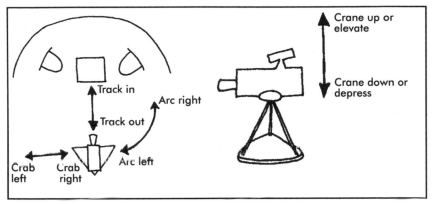

Figure 5.1(b) Camera and pedestal moves

the image. There are three controls which operate on the lens, two of them used by the Camera Operator. The one that the Camera Operator doesn't control is the iris. This is simply a variable size hole at the back of the lens to let more or less light through to the pickup device. The reason this isn't done by the Camera Operator is that it is one of the exposure controls, and the exposure of all cameras must be balanced one to another. This is done by the vision engineer whose job it is to ensure that all the cameras produce identical pictures in terms of light and colour.

The other two controls, both used by the Camera Operator, are the focus and zoom controls. The focus adjusts the distance from which the camera sees a sharp image. This is very important since the eye is naturally drawn to what is sharp in the image. The Camera Operator must therefore ensure that the key character or object in the shot is always in focus. The zoom control changes the angle at which the lens looks, so variation of it allows the Camera Operator to alter from close up to long shot. Both of these functions have remote controls on the panning handles. Sometimes those remotes have pre-set shot angles available on a set of buttons called a shot box.

When using these controls the Camera Operator needs to remember that the focus is most critical on the narrowest zoom angle, so the standard procedure is to zoom in to the closest possible shot, set the critical focus, then zoom back to get correct framing. If this is observed then as the Camera Operator zooms in (later) the focus will be held. If they try to set focus on a wide angle the shot will fall out of focus if later zoomed in.

The middle, biggest box, of the camera is where the electronic processing happens. The light from the lens, already an image, is immediately split into three components. These are the three primary colour versions of the image – red, green and blue. From these defined colours any other colour can be rebuilt. They fall onto three separate pickup devices – these days usually Charge Coupled Devices, or CCDs – and are separately processed by the camera electronics. Although there are many circuits and systems within the camera head many of their functions are controlled by the vision engineer, in the vision control area, rather than by the Camera Operator, so we will not cover them here.

The third box on the camera is the viewfinder. This is much larger than the corresponding ones on location cameras, taking advantage of the camera's relative immobility to give the Camera Operator a better indication of what they are achieving.

In the past the viewfinder has been monochrome, because the cost of colour monitors of that size and precision was not felt to be justified when the Camera Operator was primarily concerned with framing and focusing rather than colour balance, but these days studio cameras are normally fitted with colour viewfinders. The viewfinder has a hood over it to maintain picture contrast, even with light spilling onto it. The viewfinder should tilt up and down to allow the operator to see the picture comfortably when using extreme camera angles, or if the camera is at a height greater than the operator. Within the viewfinder area will be a red tally light to indicate that the camera has been chosen by the Vision Mixer as the output picture. There will be a larger tally light on top of the viewfinder to indicate to the performers that this is the output camera. This avoids the guesswork of 'which camera am I on!' Usually the Camera Operator has the option of switching other signals into their viewfinder – perhaps the main output shot, various test signals, and sometimes an overlay of their own picture with another, to aid them getting comparable framing.

Another crucial system the camera will have is some kind of talkback or intercom connecting the Camera Operator with the director in the control gallery, and possibly also with the vision engineer. This is on a headset, so that instructions can be given without interrupting performers.

In a scripted programme the Camera Operator will have a camera card listing all the shots they are required to take. A key responsibility they have is to move rapidly (when the vision mixer moves off their camera) to the next listed shot. The sooner they can get it the sooner the director can use it, even if that is a little ahead of when it's due in the programme! In an unscripted programme at least the director will have given them outline instructions of what their camera is to cover.

On the other hand when their camera is chosen by the vision mixer movement should be avoided, unless motivated. This can sometimes lead to difficulties when a director, stuck for a usable image, comes unexpectedly to a camera which hasn't got its shot quite ready. The trick here is not to make a sudden correction (which would draw attention to the error) but slowly to 'cheat' it right.

In summary then a good Camera Operator will give the director good well focused, well framed images for the maximum time possible, and will be aware all the time of their tally light!

6 The vision mixer

A television studio is a complex place, particularly the production control gallery. Lots of busy people, confusing layers of sound, and many pictures. It falls to the Vision Mixer to make sense of all the pictures by choosing the right one to go out to be recorded or transmitted, and to give the director the correct transitions between pictures, and combinations of images. The Vision Mixer has one main piece of equipment, but that is one of the most complex in the studio. Confusingly that equipment is also called a vision mixer. The Vision Mixer operates the vision mixer! From here on we will show the person as the Vision Mixer and the equipment operated the vision mixer. It is common in some countries to call the vision mixer a video switcher. As we shall see neither is quite accurate because the equipment will both switch and mix. The important thing is not what you call it, but understanding what it does.

It could be said that the Vision Mixer has relatively little chance for creative input, since what he is doing is reliably delivering, for the director, the transitions that the director has already chosen.

Whilst it is true that a good Vision Mixer will not have to think about many common transitions – like touch typing they will happen almost automatically – it is in the unusual that the challenge lies. That and the ability to react quickly, accurately, while under pressure, are what makes the job more interesting. When the director unexpectedly asks for a new title to be superimposed, or decides she is going to an unscripted reaction shot in the middle of a fast cut sequence, that is when the Vision Mixer will face a real test of their knowledge and skill.

The equipment

The vision mixer

What then is this wonder machine that the Vision Mixer operates and what does it do? Once we understand that, we can easily understand what the Vision Mixer does. They simply operate a box called the vision mixer under instruction from the director.

In very simple summary the vision mixer takes in a number of different signals (representing images) and sends out one to be recorded or transmitted. Sometimes that one is a simple repeat of one of the input signals; sometimes, not infrequently, it is a combination of two or more of them. It also allows different ways of going between the signals (or pictures). Many vision mixers will also give out 'preview' picture signals that enable the Vision Mixer to test special effects and other shots before committing them to the main output.

The pictures going in will include, at the very least, every camera in use on the programme. Additional full images which may be available could include telecine (an image from a film projector unit), telejector or slide scanner (an image from slide), stills store (an image from a library of still images held on computer disc), video source machines (for pre-recorded video sequences), a connection to another studio (or studios) to allow remote feeds, a feed from a satellite dish (to allow international connection), a feed from a video effects unit (to allow manipulated images to be used), and even perhaps a feed from a camera on a speeding Grand Prix car, or from a helicopter! Of course not all of these will be available every time – what is available, and what is to be used, depends on the studio and on the nature of the programme.

Partial images, which will be combined with others before going to output, could include such things as a VT clock, caption generator for titling, a matte generator for building layered pictures and a subtitle generator. With four, or maybe more, cameras, and possibly more than one VT source, the Vision Mixer could easily be dealing with upwards of twenty different pictures!

Vision mixer layout

The layout of vision mixers differs from machine to machine, but all of them will have columns and rows of buttons, arranged in groups. The rows

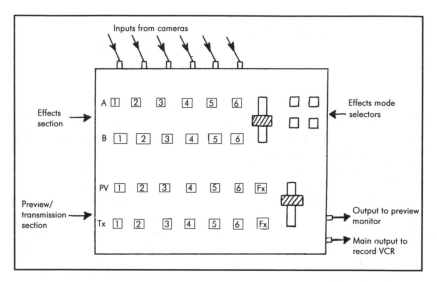

Figure 6.1   A simple vision mixer

are sometimes called banks or busses. In most there are also a number of faders. The full images, such as the cameras', come into the columns of buttons. Camera 2's buttons, for instance, will be arrayed one above each other. The Vision Mixer makes a simple selection (on any of the horizontal rows) by pressing the appropriate button, so moving left to right they might press in turn Camera 1, Camera 2, Camera 3, Camera 4, VT source 1, VT source 2, etc. The rows allow for different ways of moving between the images. So, for instance, with Camera 1 selected on the A bus, and Camera 2 on the B bus moving a fader at the end of the rows might give a mix.

The partial images such as caption generator come into separate areas, and are combined either with the pre-selected output picture or with some stage of transition before that (such as the mix mentioned above between A and B).

The different transitions available will depend on the complexity of the vision mixer, but all of them will allow the two commonest, the cut and the mix (or dissolve, or fade).

The cut gets its name from a film technique where the recording medium (the film) is physically cut and rejoined between two frames. The effect of this when played back is an instant switch between the two images.

This is achieved in a vision mixer by switching electronically between the two images, and the Vision Mixer does this very simply by pressing a different button in the group that is active.

Although this may sound a very harsh way of moving from image to image it is actually the closest to how we look at the world. In our normal experience our eyes are restless, often moving to look at different parts of the view available to us. This may be triggered by sound (somebody shouts at us, we turn to look at them) or by something that we can see (the person who we are looking at suddenly looks up, we follow their eyes to look up also). Because of the way our brain and eyes work, though, we are not aware of seeing anything whilst our eyes are moving to the new part of the scene.

It is as if we instantly move our eyes to the new position. This is an exact equivalent of what the cut gives us. The crucial thing is to get the timing of it exactly right, on the very moment when we would have wanted to move our eyes had we been looking at the scene directly. Such a well timed cut becomes almost invisible – a badly timed one will stand out as intrusive to our concentration on the scene. Luckily the timing of the cut is the responsibility of the director rather than the Vision Mixer, but the split second nature of that correct moment does mean the Vision Mixer must have quick, accurate reactions to the director's instructions.

Visual effects

Wipes and mixes
The mix (or fade or dissolve), and indeed all other transitions available on the vision mixer, is not similar to something in the natural world so has to be used with care, and only when justified by the programme. What happens is that one image will slowly fade away as another fades up to take its place. A mix must be given time to have its effect – normally a minimum time of about 2½–3 seconds is recommended, but it could be a lot longer. For an appreciable amount of time two images are laid over each other on the screen. The director needs to choose carefully images which will work together like this, remembering that for most of the time of the mix neither image will be at its full level of vividness and contrast. Some vision mixers allow for three or more images to mix together, but this rarely succeeds as the confusion of different layers of picture reduces the effectiveness of all.

The Vision Mixer executing a mix needs to be careful first to select the final image of the mix, in its appropriate group, before starting to move the fader. A mix with a cut in the middle of it (the result of selecting the final image too late) looks very messy.

Most programmes normally have at least two fades, because a nearly universal convention is that programmes start by fading up from black and finish by fading back down to it. This is just a special case mix.

Almost all vision mixers, as well as displaying indicators on their front panel, have the ability to switch indicator lights (called tally lights) on the cameras they send to output. This is a very valuable aid to the camera operators, and floor performers, showing which is the active camera. It is normal practice for a tally light to come on below the active camera monitor in the control room. This is particularly useful if two cameras are being mixed when both monitor tally lights will come on for the duration of the mix. To make sure they work accurately the Vision Mixer must ensure they are careful about, for instance, completing fader movements and positively pressing buttons.

As well as moving between pictures vision mixers allow for combinations of images to be put together. Two commonly found combinations are wipes and key effects.

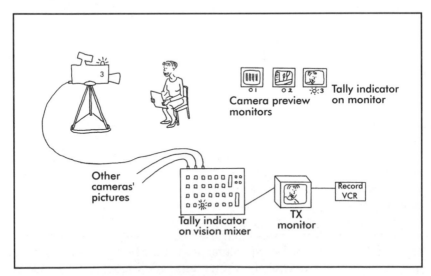

Figure 6.2   A vision mixer selecting camera to output and visible tally on camera top

Wipes simply generate a geometrical pattern – at its simplest a straight line – and put an image on each side of the line created. The line could have a coloured border added to it, or be soft, or have patterning along it. Wipes are used in two ways. Either the wipe itself is preset to a fixed position, and the complete package of the two images is then sent to output. This might be used, for example, to show both sides of a telephone conversation, or a close up shot magnifying a critical part of the action, inset into the longer shot. The other way of using wipes is to have them actually move across between images on output, but here the same constraints apply as to using a mix - it must not be too fast, and must be justified by the images. Wipes used to be very popular, but are now less favoured. Their artificiality is less acceptable to a sophisticated audience.

Keying

Key effects are a very important way of combining pictures, but here we can only give a brief introduction. There are two versions of keying – keying on brightness and keying on colour. What both do is use a triggering image to cut a hole in another picture, and then fill that hole with a third picture.

Brightness keying discriminates between two different brightnesses in, for instance, the output of a caption generator. This then derives a shape

Figure 6.3 Brightness keying

Figure 6.4   Chromakey

which in turn cuts a gap in the output picture. The gap is refilled with something else – in this case usually a plain colour. This particular technique is very commonly used to cut coloured letters (titles for example) into a pictorial image.

Colour keying (known as chromakey, or colour separation overlay) works with two rather than three images. From one picture a specified colour (often blue) is electronically removed. The part of the image that was that colour is then replaced by another image. This is a very powerful effect allowing the layering together of two images so that they look like one. This allows all sorts of impossible, dangerous, or just expensive composite shots to be built up.

Vision mixers, or video switchers (equipment), can seem intimidating and confusing when you first come to them, but the key to understanding them is to look at what is happening on the output screen, as you operate each control on its own. Also look at the indicators. Different buttons will light up, warning indicators will light up or flash. Start with simple transitions, one by one, and you will soon get the hang of it.

7 The engineering team

Each studio will have its own engineering section, to ensure that the equipment is kept running in the best order. This could be just one person in a small studio, who would be able to diagnose faults and then arrange for them to be fixed, whilst doing the routine adjustment of equipment to keep it performing in the optimum way.

The production team will also need engineering support to ensure they get the best out of the available equipment. Very often the Studio Engineer is hired (with the studio) to fulfil this role. He or she will make sure that all the studio equipment to be used is working to its best capacity for the production, before the production team arrive.

There are two main areas which need engineering for production – sound and vision. With modern equipment being much more stable than its equivalent of a decade ago, there is less need for continuous adjustment, but perhaps more possibilities for engineers offering producers new processes.

The Vision Engineer will be responsible for getting good clear images, of consistent colour and exposure, from the cameras. They will make small adjustments to the camera outputs as the production progresses, adjusting the exposure and maybe colour balance to allow for changing images.

It is a mark of a skilful Vision Engineer that all the images in a programme (though maybe coming from a variety of sources) look consistent with one another.

All studio cameras have to be 'lined up' so that the white balance and level, the black level and the colour output are all set to a known standard and are all identical to each other before they can be used in a production.

Similarly all the monitors should be aligned so that they are giving the correct colours and brightness/contrast levels. It is not easy to judge a picture properly if the monitors are all showing different colours!

Keeping a studio in good working order needs considerable amounts of routine adjustment, especially of the vision electronics. Here are some of the processes that contribute to high quality images.

Vision engineering

Monitor line-up

To line up monochrome monitors correctly it is only necessary to ensure that the range of black to white is correct. To help with this, most studios will have an electronically generated signal called, rather unsurprisingly, picture line up generating equipment (PLUGE).

The procedure is simply to feed the PLUGE signal into the monitor, turn down both brightness and contrast controls, turn up the brightness control until a picture can just be seen and then adjust the contrast control to give a normal, balanced, picture.

Colour monitors are lined up in a similar way, but with the addition of the need to check the colour accuracy. The starting point is to turn the brightness, contrast and colour controls right down. PLUGE is used to set the brightness and contrast as before. The colour is set using a special colour bars signal which has horizontal bars of colour and black and white. This bars signal may be generated from the studio line up equipment or may come from a camera which can be set to give bars as an output. The colour control is turned up until the colours look natural. As a more accurate check, it is possible to buy a standard colour bars card, which can be placed against the monitor and the colours compared.

Camera line-up

With most modern studio cameras, once lined up, most adjustments can be carried out automatically and do not change very much from day to day. What is most important is to check the white balance at the beginning of each day and, if possible, again during the day.

This is done by placing a white card, which must be evenly illuminated by white light that is at the colour temperature that will be used for the production, in front of all the cameras. The cameras should be as close together as possible so that they are all square on to the card and zoomed in to fill the viewfinder completely. The cameras can now be adjusted, using the white balance control, until the picture of the card looks pure white.

Using the actual light level that will be used during the production, each camera can now be 'shown' a grey scale card (horizontal wedges from black to white), and the white level and black level set.

Finally, by using a standard test card containing flesh tones, each camera can be checked against the other for accuracy of colour and any minor adjustments made.

It must be stressed that this is an over simplification of the process. Vision Engineers will have a range of equipment such as oscilloscopes and vector scopes to assist in the accurate measurement of the signals coming from the cameras.

Additionally there will be special equipment that will ensure that all the vision sources are locked to each other, in time, so that they all scan together. This stops any tearing or instability of the picture when switching between cameras or other sources.

Levels of maintenance

First level

The technicians will be responsible for routine maintenance and repair of all the equipment, including sound and lighting.

There are three levels of maintenance. The first level consists of an initial diagnosis of the main symptom of the fault: let's take an example of 'there is no sound coming from the sound desk'. Normally this first level of maintenance will be carried out by the operator of the particular piece of equipment.

In our example the sound supervisor will be sufficiently competent to be able to trace the fault to an area of the sound desk fairly quickly. Let's say that the fault only seems to occur when we try to use the CD player. The sound supervisor will check that the CD is actually playing, and will check, and correct as necessary, the signal's progress from the CD through a patch bay to the channel input and then to the main outputs. Nothing has actually been 'repaired', it is more a case of checking that the signal path is correct. Over 90 per cent of all faults are operator error.

Second level

Still taking our example, it may be that the sound supervisor finds that a particular channel on the desk does not work. The CD is fine if it is sent to another channel. From here the production can continue, albeit without a channel on the sound desk and the sound supervisor need do no more. When a break in recording allows, the Studio Technician will carry out the second level. First it will be established exactly where the fault lies. In our example it could be the patch bay, the patch cords or the mixer channel. Once isolated, the technician makes a decision regarding the repair of the fault. It may be something simple, for example a lead needs re-soldering or a plug needs changing, or it may be more complex like a fault in the mixer channel itself. If it can be mended, it will be.

Third level

Continuing with the example, let's say it has been found that the fault lies in the channel of the sound mixer. Third level maintenance will require removing the channel from the mixer and, using circuit diagrams, precisely locating the fault. All studios will have a policy regarding how far the technicians can go down this path.

The equipment may still be under guarantee, in which case even taking the channel out of the mixer may invalidate the guarantee. It may be policy to take the fault to a level of finding the exact circuit board, and then send it back to the manufacturer for repair, or it may be policy to do the repair and then replace, re-align if necessary, and test the equipment.

8 The floor manager team

Without wishing to insult them, Floor Managers (and their team) are like oil! When their skills are applied judiciously the machine (i.e. the studio production) will run smoothly and efficiently. Without them, for sure, the machine will sooner or later ocize up, and will always be more troublesome and less efficient. Like oil, though, incorrect application will also cause trouble!

The team consists of the Floor Manager, possibly an Assistant Floor Manager, and maybe Floor Assistants. As the division of work is principally governed by the amount of work, which is dependent on the scale of the production, small studios, and small productions, frequently have just one person – the Floor Manager – undertaking this vital responsibility, so we will look at what is to be done, rather than concentrate on who does what.

The work falls into two major areas. The first (and this is particularly important in small studios where there may not be many support staff) is the overall duty of care for the studio floor (i.e. the acting area and its adjacent rooms). The second is the requirement to relay information between the performers and the director (and maybe PA) in the control gallery, during rehearsals and recording.

The first duty is one of those that is almost impossible to describe fully, since it contains different aspects for every different studio and every different production. Let us just list some of the elements that might be looked after by the Floor Manager: the acting area, complete with set, the overall co-ordination of floor crew (including camera operators, boom operators, props assistants, lighting crew), the well-being and efficiency of all performers; and co-ordination of wardrobe and make-up personnel. All of these have to brought together into a fully co-ordinated, efficient unit ready to deliver for the director. What would the Floor Manager do with all these? Perhaps this is easier to grasp by running through some of the questions that may run through her or his mind about these things.

Questions to be answered

The acting area First is everything in it in safe workable condition? During rehearsals and recordings are the doors shut and warning lights lit, is the ventilation system switched off (if it doesn't run silently), and are any non production lights switched off? Is everything in its correct position for the programme?

The set Is it safely constructed, with no hazards for the people moving about it? Are doors, windows, furniture all in their correct starting positions?

The crew Are they all there? Where appropriate have they got their talkback headphones on? If any crew are not yet in studio where are they? Have they all got their correct equipment, and is it working? Have things like ladders, cables, floor monitors been tidied out of possible camera sight, and away from walkways.

The performers Obviously key people in the programme. Are they either on set, in the studio standing by, or in their green room ready for a call when required? Are they fully informed about what is wanted from them, and things like where the toilets are? Are they clear about when they will be needed? Do the wardrobe team understand which costumes are needed when, and how much time they have for changes? Do the make-up team know what order the performers appear in, and when the first will be required? Are any props being used properly prepared, safe and in their correct position?

As well as this an oversight of security and safety procedures within the studio environment falls to the Floor Manager. She or he should know exactly who is in the studio, and ensure they are fully briefed on house rules. They should be fully informed about fire evacuation procedures and where to find first aid. It seems like a huge amount of work, but what is really needed is an attentive, careful attitude, checking (maybe by simply looking around the studio) that all is well, combined with the ability to communicate information clearly to everyone, to reassure them, and make sure they are fully ready to deliver when required.

Communication

The second main responsibility is to act as a channel of communication between the director and gallery crew and the performers. More often than not performers are not part of the talkback circuit. Even with miniature earpieces there are few programmes where it is appropriate for performers to have them. They are required to deliver very precise actions and speeches, perhaps time after time as technical problems are sorted out, yet still make it look fresh and spontaneous for the recording. They have bright (and hot) lights shining at them, cameras looking at them, microphones listening to them, and an unseen number of crew members out there. Perhaps even an audience expecting to be amused by them. Naturally they can get apprehensive, or downright terrified.

Upstairs in the gallery we have the director, getting steadily more frustrated as the expensive time ticks away, technical problems mounting, and still the actors cannot get their lines correct! Naturally she or he gets bad tempered.

Between these two sources of extreme and increasing tension there is the Floor Manager. Earlier we called her the oil, now perhaps you can see why. Communication is essential – the performers must be accurately told what is required of them, and, very importantly, when the problem is not with them. The director needs to be informed about the particular problems the performers are having. Delicacy and diplomacy are obviously essential, yet so is not getting in the way of real authority and urgency when necessary.

During early stages of rehearsals much of the communication could be verbal, but later the microphones would pick up the voice of the Floor Manager, so the information has to be relayed visually. This gives the Floor Manager another problem. They must get into the eyeline of the performer where it naturally falls (nothing looks worse than an unmotivated eye flick from the performer as they look for a cue), but obviously out of sight of the active camera (a long shot sees a lot of the studio). They

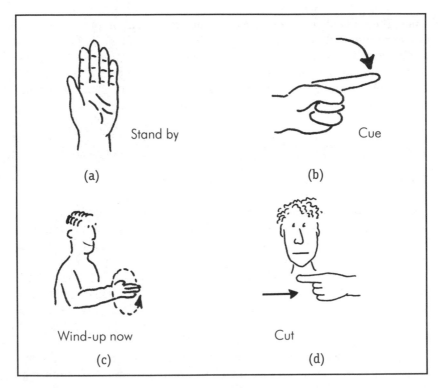

Figure 8.1   (a) Standby signal; (b) Cue signal; (c) Wind up signal; (d) cut signal

also have to be close enough to the performer to be visible against the dazzling wall of light. From this position a visual cue can be given. It must be clear and unmistakable.

Floor manager signals

There is a complete code of different signals that a Floor Manager can give, but as this is a book about basics we give here just enough to start and end the programme. The first comes in two parts! It is the signal to start (the next action, or speech). The first stage of it is the standby, see Figure 8.1a. The second is the actual cue, shown in Figure 8.1b. The second signal, also in two parts, is the wind up (time is running out), see Figure 8.1c, this is followed by the cut (the end!), Figure 8.1d.

9 The scenery team

The scenery team will consist of all the people responsible for the scenery and stages that make up the set, as well as all the movable items contained within them. These items contained within the sets are known as props (short for property). Examples of props would be chairs, tables, glasses, telephones, table lights, etc.

Often the team will be split into sections, such as the building section and the property section, all working under the Set Designer.

You can see why we say that video production is a team effort. The Set Designer has the overall responsibility for ensuring that the cameras are given as realistic a picture that the programme demands as possible, even if this means building a room in a house or a whole village!

Obviously the complexity of the department is dictated by the size and normal use of the studio. Often those in small training studios, such as those found in universities and colleges, will have little more than a few willing and industrious students who may be part of another team, perhaps even the performers, building a small set and filling it with personal possessions.

These smaller scale studios may have nothing more than a props cupboard filled with little items that have been accumulated over several years of productions. The essential requirement is a sense of order where the very minimum demand is a book containing a list of all the available items, where they are stored and who is using them.

Normally, but not always, smaller items of personal props, such as watches, spectacles and jewellery will be kept with the Wardrobe Team in a separate locked cupboard.

The scene dock

Larger studios will have a more sophisticated area which will include a scene dock. This is an area where all the scenery and sets for a particular production can be stored. The scene dock will be close to, and have easy access to, the studio floor area. Often there will be access to the outside of the building to allow for large items to be brought in, such as motor vehicles.

Associated with the scene dock will be a workshop area, where the scenery can be constructed and painted. We can see that the size and complexity of this area is very variable. There may be several carpenters, painters and other trades all working under the set designer, or there may just be a storeman/handyman.

However small scale the studio is, there will always be a need for some kind of set to be used. There is an absolute limit to the uses of just a cyclorama curtain. Even a studio interview needs some chairs, a table and perhaps some water and glasses. Remember that your production will succeed only if the visual you present to the audience is perceived as realistic.

Even the smallest studio should have a few flats, and a small amount of everyday props, stored somewhere that is easily accessible and ready for use. The best pictures from your camera team and the best sound from your sound team will count for nothing if the audience cannot imagine where they are, and what they are supposed to be looking at. Only in radio can you get away with a performer talking about their surroundings!

The props storeroom

The props store, again, is variable in size depending on the studio size and complexity. Small-scale video studios will always have a need for the odd little bits of furniture, telephones, flower vases, bottles and glasses and so on. Normally a large cupboard will suffice for the small prop items but larger items like tables and chairs, a bed and perhaps a carpet or some rugs will need to be stored somewhere. In larger complexes there will be a dedicated property storeroom with all manner of items carefully stored and labelled. There will be a storeman and probably a couple of people working with him. Very large complexes will often have a property buyer who is responsible for buying, or hiring, special props that are required for a particular production. Often these buyers are specialists who are in touch with large companies and manufacturers who will lend items such as computers, cars, watches and household items free, in return for a credit at the end of the programme.

Types of props

With large-scale props stores it is helpful to have separate areas for the different types of props. There are many different types of props but the three most often used classifications are: personal props, dressing props and action props. Personal props include all the things that are used by the performers. In this category would be things like spectacles, pens and watches. Dressing props are props that are used to dress the set and are used as decorations to the set. Curtains, cushions, ornaments and rugs are examples. The final category are the action props. These include items to be used as part of the action of the programme. Things like telephones, guns and tennis rackets are examples.

Because of the need for the scenery and props teams to work together, both will come under the overall charge of the set designer although both may have their own head of section.

10 The wardrobe team

With any studio based video production, there is a pattern that will be followed. It is obvious that there will be a requirement for some lighting so that the cameras can see, and give pictures to the director. There must be some attention given to sound so that we can hear what is going on. There must be a way of selecting the picture to be recorded (vision mixing).

Particularly true of small-scale television, and often the last consideration, is that all this action must appear to take place somewhere and it is just assumed that performers will be involved.

We have seen that scenery needs to be constructed and placed appropriately within the acting area as a set design, and that the necessary props are collected and placed within the scene. Everything is now ready for the performers. This is an area which can make a production look very poor, or can lift a mediocre performance from the actors into something that becomes acceptable because the whole performance of the production appears professional. This is the responsibility of the wardrobe team.

Wardrobe problems

People
It is only in large-scale productions and in large studios that specialist teams can be afforded to look after the performers' costumes and make-up.

Normally the performers themselves will choose, and wear, their own clothing and will attempt their own make-up with little or no knowledge of the final effect when seen on camera. Whose responsibility it is to help guide the performers in their choice is open to debate, but it will often fall to the floor manager team or the PA.

A little understanding and guidance can go a long way towards making the performers feel more professional. For this reason it is worth looking at a few technical problems.

Technical problems

Exposure

The wardrobe team need to be very well aware of the problems associated with the capabilities of the camera. Unlike our eyes, cameras work on a limited contrast range. They cannot see great ranges of white to black. The vision engineers can make some small corrections to the absolute level of white or black but they cannot alter the overall range. This means that an adjustment could be made to give correct exposure to a very white blouse, but at the expense of making a dark grey skirt appear black. Equally it follows that a dark grey skirt within the picture could be adjusted to appear dark grey, but a white blouse would now be overexposed and 'wash out'.

Another common problem is caused by inappropriate clothing. A perfectly acceptable costume seen in long shot may not be as acceptable in close up, for instance with low neckline clothing which may produce a topless effect and lead to large areas of pale coloured skin becoming over exposed.

Colour

Cameras also do not reproduce all the colours that we can see absolutely as we see them. Reds, for instance, tend to stand out as much brighter and more intrusive.

The scanning process used within the camera to convert images into television pictures leads to other problems. Certain patterns used within suits, for instance, will cause unwelcome and distracting strobe effects.

Difficulties can occur with clothing colours that match the background and tend to merge into it, losing the effect of depth between the performer and the background.

The wardrobe team need to be informed if any video special effects are intended to be used within the programme. Chroma-key is the classic example. It is possible, with technical adjustments, for a particular colour to be selected and then replaced with some totally different picture. This colour is normally blue, but it is possible to create this effect with any colour. There are occasions when this may be used for effect, in pop videos for example, to replace a shirt with moving images that 'appear' to be dancing across the performer's body, but more usually it is used as background replacement. Here a newscaster or weather forecast presenter could have images superimposed behind them. This effect would be ruined if the presenter was wearing the selected chroma colour!

Light

The wardrobe team need to know what sort of lighting is being used, and from which direction it is coming from. Some materials can become translucent allowing light to pass through, others can become totally transparent with consequent embarrassment to the performer.

Light is not reflected uniformly off all surfaces. A shiny suit, for example, may look perfectly acceptable under normal light conditions, but put it in a studio and it may look over bright and cause problems for the exposure of the cameras. Sequins and jewellery are other examples where unwanted light reflections may be cast onto the face or into the camera causing bright spots.

11 The make-up team

Working closely with wardrobe, and often part of it, is the make-up team. In small-scale television this again is normally left to the performer and the results are, at best, not good and often a disaster. This is another area where a knowledge of what the camera actually sees is essential. In broad terms there are two types of make-up, corrective and artistic.

Corrective make-up

It is essential that the make-up area of a studio has proper lighting. Studio productions take place in a closed environment, lit by tungsten lighting of a particular colour temperature. The colour temperature of this lighting is used to balance the cameras so that they believe that the light is white.

The level of light used is higher than that normally encountered in a normal room and often harder. The effect of this is that what we see under normal light conditions is not the same as the camera will see under studio lighting conditions.

Studio lighting can be simulated in a make-up area by using a large number of tungsten light bulbs fitted around a large mirror. Fluorescent lighting will produce a much softer effect and cannot approximate either the colour temperature of what the camera will actually see, nor the shadow effect. It is this shadow effect, and the effect of bright lights, that are needed to begin corrective make-up.

Corrective make-up is used to make the performer look as they would in a normal environment. Particularly obvious areas that need attention are shiny bald patches, shadows from a beard line and skin marks from, for example, bra straps. In normal lighting, natural bags under the eyes may not be noticed, but with studio lighting large, unacceptable shadows may form. If we see people in the natural environment none of these things appear important, but a close up from a video camera is very cruel. Very slightly red noses and a small bald patch will stand out like beacons if not corrected. The real trick is to cover up all these little problems without making the performer look as if they are made up.

Artistic make-up

This type of make-up is designed to 'shape' the performer into a character. It is very skilful and needs to be done by an expert make-up artist.

The character may need a scar that requires ageing as the performance progresses, or a tattoo that can be washed off later. There may be a need for a wig. The blending of a wig with the natural face so that it becomes invisible in close up is a very skilled job. Clothing may need to be made up to show blood stains.

Artistic make-up artists will need to pay particular attention to continuity. During a production day in studio it is possible for the character to have to undergo several changes that actually take place over days or weeks. An example would be that we see a character fall in the kitchen in the morning and see the character with a developing bruise at work during the day. The production day may then leave several actual days out and the character is next seen at home fully restored to health.

Artistic make-up artists often find it helpful to have a polaroid type camera to capture the size and position of these wounds so that they can be accurately reproduced and 'healed'.

The hairdresser

Working closely with the wardrobe and make-up team will often be a hairdresser. Again, in small-scale television this is often left to the actual performers. Even with small-scale television there is a need for performers to 'do their hair' and, with this in mind, the minimum requirement for a dressing room should involve some facility for washing and drying hair as well as facilities for make-up and a full length mirror to check costumes.

For large-scale productions, particularly period drama, hairdressers and stylists are essential. Wigs will almost inevitably be used and these need careful storage and handling if they are to look consistently the same, day after day. Many professional performers have become very adept at fitting and grooming their own wigs for the theatre. Television is a totally different matter. It is the nature of television, and film, that any small discrepancy will be instantly noticed.

If a production is to last several days, or is part of a series, performers must look consistent. A large part of television uses close up images. Unlike the theatre the camera directs us to look at the image presented to us by the director. Hair tends to appear to grow at an alarming rate if viewed in close up. Because the picture of the performer's head and shoulders is dominant any small change in length or shape becomes much more accentuated.

It is normally sufficient to keep the hair constantly trimmed so as not to draw attention to it at all. Sometimes, however, it needs to be seen to have grown or have been cut. Judging the actual amount of growth, or cut, that is acceptable on camera, and in close up, is a specialist skill.

12 A little paperwork

Conceptualization

It is important to remember that a television programme is an audiovisual experience. This means that the whole thing must be thought out in both sound and picture. Programmes will not work if either is thought of in isolation. It is never a success to try and fit sound to existing pictures or pictures to existing sound. The only exception to this is possibly the pop video where the song exists first, then pictures are fitted to reflect the mood or theme of the song. Sometimes this works reasonably well, but attempting it is a specialist skill.

We will take two examples to show how a programme idea may develop. The first one is a location section. This may well become an insert into a studio programme, for instance as a scene setter to a studio debate. It may be a complete programme in its own right. Whatever its final form it will still need to be taken through all the stages outlined in this chapter on 'A little paperwork'.

The second example is for a studio drama programme. We have assumed, in the example, that the early stages, outlined for the location shoot, have been completed and the procedure has been picked up at the storyboard stage.

Aims

The programme must have some sort of aim, without an aim it will wander 'aimlessly'. The aim is an initial idea, often quite vague in nature along the lines of, for instance, 'we will do a programme on pollution'. The importance of an aim is that it gives something to focus on, a starting point, we now know the programme will concern itself with pollution. This germ of an idea gives us the concept of the programme which can be stated as an aim; 'We will do something on pollution'.

Objectives

The next stage is to write down some objectives – these are precise statements of intent. To take our example, pollution is so vast a subject that we need to select an area or areas that the programme will concentrate on. We need to set time limits for the programme. We need to define the type of programme – is this a serious documentary or a comedy, for instance. Above all we need to define the content. We might end up with a statement such as 'We will do a 30 minute documentary drama about the effects on fish of industrial waste leaking into our rivers. The programme will show the effect on fish stocks and will heighten awareness of the problem with a view to making industry more responsible over their treatment of the environment.'

From our idea, or aim, we have now moved to a much more precise statement of what the programme is about. The precision of our objective is such that it is measurable. This means that we can test whether the programme met its objective. As a result of watching the programme was industry more aware of the problem? Did industry takes steps to be more responsible? Only if we have an objective and we test it through the results of the programme can we really say whether the programme was a success or not.

Target audience

At this stage we need to define who this programme is aimed at. The whole structure of the programme and its language and images must be fitted around a particular group of people. If a programme is intended for children, for instance, the visual and aural language will be much simpler than if the programme was aimed at university professors. Defining the target audience will keep our minds on who we are making the programme for. In our example we are trying to heighten awareness with a view to make industry more responsible. Who is industry? Are we doing this programme for the directors of industrial companies? Is this a specialist programme with a very limited target audience? Are we only concerned with people who work in industry? Is this a social problem that we want to bring to everybody's attention? Who do we want to influence? Whose 'awareness needs heightening'? Are we aiming to bring this problem to everybody in order that pressure groups can be formed and, maybe, legislation is introduced to prevent the problem? If we had used a more precise objective and said that this was going to be a 'public awareness' programme then maybe the target audience would have been easier to define.

Both the objective and the target audience really go together and need thinking about together. If the two are too rigorously structured it becomes easy to lose any creativity that may be brought to the programme. An easy approach is to start off by thinking about what we want to do and to whom. This can then be tightened up at a later stage.

The treatment

We have now got the basic idea of the programme, we know the area we are working in (the aim). We know precisely which aspect we will deal with (the objective). We know who we are expecting to watch the programme (the target audience). What we don't know is how are we going to do it.

The treatment of a programme is the beginning of its creation. The treatment will state how the programme will take shape. All the ideas we had when we were thinking about the programme can now be brought together into a simple document which follows the programme from opening to end.

The treatment is a very important stage in the production process. Normally when a client is involved and we have been asked to make a programme for that client, the aim, objective and target audience will have been supplied. We will be asked to go away and come up with a treatment. This gives the client a basic working document which shows precisely how we are going to do his or her programme. It is neither a script (but the script will come from the treatment), nor a visualization (but the pictures and sound will also come from the treatment).

To help in the construction of a treatment it is necessary to have lots of ideas about the programme written down, ideas about the type of music, ideas about the type of shots, ideas about the type of words to be spoken, ideas about the type of performers, ideas about the types of locations and so on.

The treatment will pull all of these together in a logical order so that the client can get the overall feel of the programme. This makes it a lot easier to discuss precise areas of script or precise locations that will be part of the programme.

If we stay with our imaginary programme, the treatment might start out by saying:

The programme opens with a typical country scene, sound effects of birds singing and soft, gentle music add to the visual of a long shot of the countryside with a river meandering through the meadows with a small wood in the distance, to give a feeling of peace and security contained within the countryside.

Already we have the opening feel of the programme, we can 'see' the images and imagine the complementary sounds. The precise location is not necessary, what is needed is an overall view of how the programme starts.

The treatment might go on:

As the camera moves closer to the river, anglers can be seen quietly fishing from the bank. As the music fades, we cut to see that two middle-aged anglers are having a conversation. The conversation is based around the lack of fish and the bad state of the water, there is reminiscing of their childhood days when they swam in the river and there were lots of anglers catching lots of fish.

This has a suggestion in sound and picture that all is not well, there is a memory of better days, there is a suggestion that the water is no longer clean.

There is also a suggestion of what is happening with the visuals: we started with a long shot, zoomed in to the river and cut to the anglers. There is the suggestion of the type of conversation that goes with these images, not precise words but enough for us to recognize the sort of conversation and the sort of mood being created.

It might go on:

One angler points up river and says 'I blame it on the new factory', the picture cuts to the factory belching smoke from its chimneys in mid shot, beside the river.

This has given us a change of mood and a logical cut, led by the angler pointing to the culprit. The whole opening bit of this imagined treatment has covered everything the client will want to know. How are we going to do his programme? What sort of visuals will we use? What sort of sounds are there? What sort of performers are involved? How are we going to start?

It also gives a starting point for the dialogue that will follow when we sit down with the client and discuss the programme. Often a client will have ideas for the programme that, perhaps, haven't yet quite formed. The problem we are faced with is how do we get the ideas out of the client's head and into our treatment. It may be that the client will like the opening but, for example, want it reversed. Start with the factory and then go to the anglers talking. There is enough flexibility in the treatment to have things moved around, or added to. Nothing is yet fixed. The ideas have been put on paper and communicated. The treatment has shown how we are going to 'treat' the programme. What is important is that the whole thing has been described in sounds and pictures to build up an idea of how we are going to make this programme.

The storyboard

Once the treatment has been agreed the next stage is to do the visualization. This will involve a storyboard, script and, finally, camera cards. As explained earlier we will take a studio example for these next three stages. Assume that the aims, objectives, target audience and treatment have already been completed.

The storyboard has a series of still images drawn in boxes in the video ratio that will be used for shooting. This is normally 4 x 3, but, with advancing technology, increasingly Wide Screen format is being used. This is a new ratio of 16 x 9. You will probably have seen some of these programmes on television already. If you have a standard 4 x 3 television set then the picture will look like a letterbox slot in the middle of the screen. Wide screen sets are becoming very common in the 'home movie' market and make the 16 x 9 picture look like the film equivalent of 'Cinemascope'.

As well as these boxes of the pictures, either to the right or below, will be an area for the script. The boxes will be numbered, in the top left-hand corner, and these numbers refer to the shot number. The still images are a pictorial representation of the beginning of each shot. If the shot develops (pans or zooms for example) an instruction to that effect will be written in. Only when the shot changes do we need to draw another image. There may be another number on the top right-hand corner which will be used later to indicate which camera will be responsible for that shot. Sometimes the script

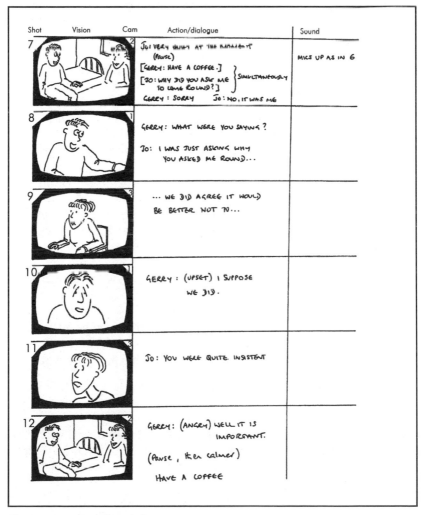

Figure 12.1   Storyboard shots

is only written as the first and last line, but in this case there should be a full script kept separately. More normally the whole script is written beside each shot. Any music or sound effects are put in a separate column after the script.

The storyboard is the first time that the actual sound and pictures are put together in visual form. It is also the last time, because other documents will now be used that only give sound information or only picture information. The storyboard is the last check the client will have before being committed to the expensive process of production.

The storyboard marks a very important stage in the production planning. It is not only at this stage that a representation of the actual programme can be seen, but it is often the stage at which the client will be expected to pay part of the programme fee.

Minor changes may be made to the programme once the storyboard has been approved, but anything major will involve the client in more money. For this reason alone the storyboard must be an accurate representation of precisely what is going to be seen and heard.

The storyboard is the responsibility of the scriptwriters who will have visualization artists working with them. Very often, because of the obvious differences between a theatre production and a television production, the scriptwriter is known as the screenwriter. Whichever title they use it is important that they are fully aware of the television process and what is, and is not, possible with cameras and, particularly, when to use which size of shot. Although the final decision during production is the director's, the whole programme has to be conceived at this stage as accurately as possible to its finished form.

Looking at the diagram you will see what a typical storyboard will look like. We have only taken shots seven to twelve as examples because we will also use them to transfer these to a script listing and a camera card.

The script

Once we have the storyboard approved, we can translate it to the shooting script. This is similar to the storyboard but without the pictures. On the left-hand side are the shot number and written instructions about the shot using the known abbreviations. The middle of the page is given over to the words, and any instructions for performers. The right-hand side will have notes for the sound team about music or effects. At the appropriate point in the script there will be a horizontal line with a slash mark to indicate the cutting point.

Whereas the storyboard was a document, generated for the client, that showed the programme in words and pictures, the script is the first of the 'technical' documents designed for use by the director and the various teams in the production.

If you look at Figure 12.2, a typical script, you can see that shot 7 is a 2 shot of the two performers (Gerry and Jo) and the words spoken are 'Very quiet at the moment,' and so on. The camera cuts to the next shot (shot 8

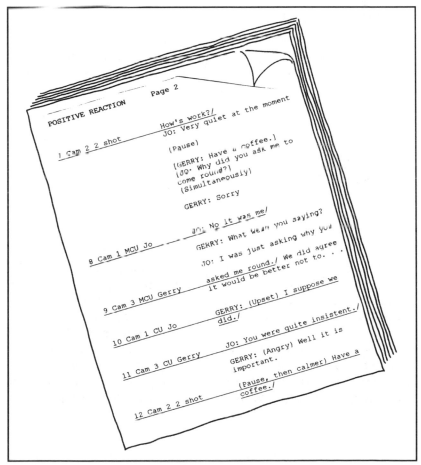

Figure 12.2   A script layout

on camera 1), which is a Medium Close Up (MCU) of Jo, at the slash mark after 'me'. You will also see that Gerry 'Have a coffee'. and Jo 'Why did you ask me round?' are in square brackets, this indicates a stage direction which is explained under the lines by 'simultaneously'.

After the Medium Close Ups from Cameras 1 and 3 (shots 8 and 9), both cameras move to a Close Up (CU) in shots 10 and 11.

At this stage of the script there are no special instructions for sound, which would appear on the right hand side of the page.

Camera cards

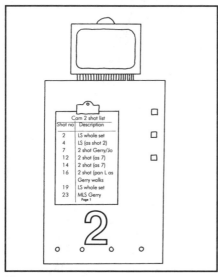

Figure 12.3   Camera 2 Shot list

From the script the director and the camera team will work out which camera will be responsible for which shot. Individual cameras are not concerned with what the other cameras are doing or what sound is doing, all they need is a simple list of which shot numbers they are responsible for and what type of shot it is. There is a diagram showing a typical camera card for camera 2 for the script we showed earlier and you can see that the camera has some establishing long shots (LS) at the beginning (shots 2 and 4), then tightens into a 2 shot (both performers) to follow the interaction between the two performers (shots 7, 12 and 14). When they stand up, and Gerry walks out, the camera has a movement as it pans left to accommodate the movement of Gerry (shot 16). The camera goes back to its Long Shot (LS) at shot 19 and has a Medium Long Shot (MLS) of Gerry as its final shot (shot 23).

13 Single camera production

A large part of this book has been taken up with studio production. A great deal of what has been said about the roles of the various teams, and the equipment they use to do their job, is directly transferable to single camera production. To avoid repetition, we will now only concentrate on the differences between studio and single camera production, assuming you will go back if you need more explanation.

Whereas a studio production uses a multi-camera set up, with any necessary video inserts, and chooses the images to be recorded using the vision mixer to produce a linear programme, single camera production takes a totally different approach.

The most obvious difference is that, whereas a studio is an enclosed, controllable space, if only one camera is being used it becomes highly portable. Often single camera production is shortened to PSC, or portable single camera. Because the camera can go practically anywhere, special skills will be needed by all the team members. To go 'on location' could mean anything from shooting in an office to shooting under the sea.

Without the back-up of the studio engineering team, the fixed environment and, often, mains electricity, the lighting and sound teams, particularly, need to rethink their whole strategy. There are three basic stages to go through. The first is the acquisition stage, where all the shots, inserts, captions and graphics needed for the programme are collected together onto many tapes. The order that these are collected in is one of convenience, not one of a linear nature. The second stage is the editing stage where the whole programme is cut together into its linear order and any special effects transitions are added. The third stage is the audio post-production stage where any additional audio, music, effects or voiceover, are added.

The process is entirely different from studio production and requires a different type of planning. The programme will only be a success if you plan to 'shoot to edit'. This involves considerable continuity skills as well as involving the PA in keeping track of not only where we are in the script, but also, more importantly, where we are in relation to what went before and what follows.

The acquisition stage

Before we look at the specific roles of the teams, and their equipment, we will break the stages down. Acquisition is the word we use for gathering together all the elements of the programme. Whatever recorded format we will eventually end up with is irrelevant at this stage, what is important is to get the very best quality of picture and sound recorded onto something. For small-scale production this will normally mean recording onto Hi8 or S-VHS format. Increasingly one of the high-end domestic or the semi-professional digital formats is becoming popular as the cost falls and the range increases. The DV format is one such example which has been derived from the professional DVCAM system. The main difference lies in a limited audio capability and the omission of an in-camera editing system whereby the first frame of each shot is stored in memory to make for easier access at the editing stage.

Increasingly there is an overlap between the consumer (domestic) market and the low-budget corporate market. Modern Hi8 camcorders will offer shooting in either 4 x 3 or wide screen format and the DV format ensures the highest possible quality with minimal loss of quality when copied.

For larger scale, more expensive, acquisition film or the much more expensive professional, digital formats are used because of their superior picture quality.

If the acquisition is on video, the equipment used to get the various shots, regardless of the format used, will be one of three types.

The most common is a camcorder. This is a camera and recorder, all in one case, and with a microphone fitted to it. This is a sort of 'one person shooting kit'. It is often possible to plug in a separate microphone, so the on-camera microphone does not have to be used if it is deemed unsuitable for a particular shot. It is also possible to output a signal to a monitor, and maybe to clip a small light onto the camera hotshoe.

A second type has a separate camera and video recorder. The advantage with this arrangement is that, as well as finding it lighter, the camera person can get on with the job of a camera operator without having to look after videotape operation and sound. The disadvantage is that leads are needed to connect the camera and the microphone to the videotape recorder, resulting in a team of two or three people having to move about together as if in a three-legged race!

The third option, and one that is becoming more popular, is to have a 'dockable' recorder. This involves the same set-up as the second option (a separate camera and video recorder), but with the added advantage that, whilst they are two separate pieces of equipment, the recorder can be plugged directly into the back of the camera. Depending on the shot that is required, the system can be operated as a camcorder or as a separate recorder and camera. This gives the director a great deal of flexibility.

Because of the problem of shooting out of sequence, it is not possible to judge exactly what will finally cut to what. No matter how carefully the shots have been planned there will always be an awkward moment at the edit stage when we need something in between two shots to make the transition more acceptable.

For this reason it is essential that as many different 'cut-aways' as possible are recorded at each location. These could be anything from a close up, a crowd scene, a general traffic scene to a long shot of the area. Anything that could be used, later, to help get from one shot to another without it being obvious to the viewer.

To help with the sound transitions, and to create the general atmosphere of where the action is taking place, it is equally important that the sound team collect as much background sound as possible. This should be recorded separately from any dialogue, onto a different tape if possible, so that it can be mixed with the programme sound at the edit or post-production stage. This extra sound is known as 'Buzz Track' or 'Atmos'.

The dialogue sound is normally recorded onto one or more of the audio tracks of the video recorder to maintain synchronization with the pictures. Increasingly these days timecode will be recorded at the same time. The full use of timecode will be dealt with when we look at the editing and post production stages but, for the moment, it is sufficient to say that this is a code which records a unique identification number onto each frame as it is shot. This gives the possibility of finding any frame accurately, each and every time, at a later stage.

If film is used for acquisition, or if the sound is to be recorded separately, for instance onto a DAT recorder, then timecode must be recorded.

Normally at the acquisition stage, but sometimes during post production, any graphics or captions will be made and collected onto a computer disc. At the acquisition stage the PA will be kept very busy logging (writing down) each and every take of each shot with notes detailing whether the sound, picture, or both are useable. This log should be such that, at a later stage, any useable shot can be found quickly, together with its running time. If timecode is being used this becomes a fairly easy job, if not, several stopwatches will be needed.

The editing stage

Once all the shots have been gathered together, it is possible to assemble them into the correct order and complete the programme. This is done at the editing stage. Film editing involves actually cutting the film and sticking the bits together to form a finished product. With video this is no longer done (although it was in the very early days of video production).

Editing involves either copying the relevant shots, in a linear order, from the original tapes onto a new tape to make the finished product, or loading the original tape into a computer and manipulating the images in a non linear fashion: cutting, pasting and changing sections before finally putting it all in the right order and then copying it back to tape.

Editing is looked at in much more depth later. Here we are only concerned with an overview. The stages that need to be gone through are to make sure that all the shots are logged. This should have been done by the PA during the shooting, but if the logs are incomplete they must be completed now. It helps to start with a paper edit, this involves referring back to the storyboard and ensuring that all the shots actually do exist and that they will cut together. It is here that the need for cutaways will become obvious.

The next stage involves what is known as 'off line' editing. This will normally be done by copying the original tapes onto a lower format and using a cheaper editing suite to make a rough cut edit. If timecode was used in the original shoot, this is copied at the same time, but burnt into the picture so that it can be seen. This 'burnt in timecode' is talked about in edit suites as BITC.

Cheaper formats are used because this 'off line' stage takes the longest, and we don't need to spend hours in an expensive edit suite trying edits and producing a rough cut.

Once we are happy with the rough cut edit, the timecode numbers and the original tapes can go to an 'on line' edit suite where the actual edit will take place. The resulting copy will be produced on a high quality format (often digital), to preserve the quality needed to produce the final copies.

Often this on line edit can be done automatically, because the timecode numbers can be put into a form known as an edit decision list (EDL) which are fed into a computer that runs the machines. This process is known as auto-conforming.

The post-production stage

Finally the master tape may go to a post-production suite where the audio can be finished, and any computer generated graphics or animation can be fitted into gaps that were left in the tape earlier.

Health and safety

Shooting on location brings a whole new set of problems on the Health and Safety front. A great deal of what was discussed earlier when we looked at Health and Safety in the studio is directly transferable to location shooting, but there are new areas to be considered.

However much planning is done and however careful people are, accidents can happen. For this reason whenever location shooting takes place insurance is a vital requirement.

By law all companies must have Public Liability Insurance to cover any accident caused to the public. Most clients will require even freelance operators to provide insurance for at least one million pounds of public liability.

For simplicity we will consider location shooting in two categories. One is indoors, the other is outdoors.

Indoors

Indoor shooting can best be described as working in a temporary single camera studio. The main consideration comes from the fact that this studio is a temporary affair and has to be constructed for the shoot and then dismantled. Often the working space will be very small and the need for care when moving around cannot be over emphasized.

Power requirements will all come from the existing, often domestic, mains supply. If a 1 kW lamp is used it will take nearly 5 amps from a 230 volt supply. More than two cannot be sensibly plugged into the supply in one room. To do so risks, at best, blowing fuses and at worst the possibility of an electrical fire.

The lights themselves will necessarily have long trailing cables and will normally be mounted on flimsy, lightweight, stands mounted on the floor. This gives rise to an obvious safety hazard. You should be aware of the high heat output from these lights and remember that these lights will be operating in confined spaces at low level. It is a very wise precaution to have a suitable fire extinguisher close to the shooting and particularly important to know where the electrical isolator is sited.

Because portable shooting crews consist of a very few people there will not be a floor manager. For this reason someone needs to be delegated to look after the safety of performers and to make sure that they do not go near trailing cables or lights.

Outdoors

Applicable to both studio and indoor operations, but left until now because of the larger consideration of outdoor shooting, are the legal requirements under an EC Directive on Health and Safety at Work.

Employers are required to make a suitable and sufficient assessment of the risks to the health and safety of employees to which they are exposed whilst they are at work. Similarly they are required to make an assessment of the risks to people not employed by them, i.e. the general public or performers that may be used or connected with the programme. Similar regulations apply to the self employed.

There are many things that could constitute a hazard to health and safety, but the most common are: electricity, lighting, fire, contact with hot surfaces, falling objects and, particularly on location, confined spaces, adverse weather, excavations and moving vehicles. When the location crews move out into the street whole new problems arise. The safety of the public becomes even more important. Inevitably a television crew attracts attention, the general public become curious and must be expected to come and watch. Apart from the fact that the crew are responsible for their safety, there is a risk of falling foul of the law by causing an obstruction.

Apart from the law concerning Health and Safety Regulations, all local authorities will have their own laws which will affect what can and cannot be done. Permission is normally required to film in any public place, including parks. Individual police forces, too, will have regulations regarding the use of pseudo emergency vehicles, emergency service clothing, the use of firearms, the positioning and use of lights and anything that might endanger the public.

You should never assume that you can shoot anything you want anywhere. Examples of the most often forgotten need for permission include the fact that most churches will not automatically allow any filming inside. Even if it is allowed there have been cases where production companies have fallen foul of the law because of the neglected clearance of copyright for the organ music. The London Underground have very strict rules concerning shooting on their property or trains, a cost is normally involved as well as specific written permission. So called 'public' parks do not carry an automatic right to shoot, some will not allow the erection of a tripod even with permission to shoot.

In the case of street interviews, you will have to contend with people who are completely ignorant of the television process and you must ensure their safety.

The crew may also require some safety protection. For example, a common requirement is for a camera operator to follow a performer up (or down) steps – certainly a hazardous procedure, and maybe a potential accident. Something as simple as another crew member physically holding on to the camera person to guide them may make this less dangerous. Often inventiveness and ingenuity can provide simple answers to apparently lethal situations! It should be an integral part of the initial recce for a shoot to assess any possible danger, and plan to avoid it.

Remember as well that environmental considerations come into play in this area. What looks like a great shot – the dramatically blazing oil tanker

– could be completely unacceptable (and maybe even seriously illegal) from the pollution point of view. It is probably a good idea to seek specialist safety and ecological advice for such programmes.

14 The Director and PA on location

On location, with a portable single camera (PSC) shoot, the Director is just as busy and the PA still has much to do. Both of them are just as pivotal to the programme's success as their equivalents in studio.

Pre-production

In the stage before shooting much of the preparatory work required on studio productions still has to be done. The Director will still be involved with the development of the shooting script, planning camera angles, casting then rehearsing performers, schedules planning.

Each of these will be different in emphasis from the similar studio based process. The shooting script is no longer limited to what can be shot in a reasonably sized, reasonably priced set. Any setting is now possible, but there is still a financial constraint. Tempting as it may be to plan a week's shooting in the Bahamas the cost of transporting crew, performers and equipment to such an exotic destination would rule it out for most programmes. The cheapest productions are the ones that involve the minimum of travel. A wise Director will not only keep the travel costs down by working close to base, but will also be inventive about how perhaps quite small areas of locations can be cheated to look as the programme needs – just because you're out on location doesn't mean every shot is a long shot.

In planning camera angles the Director now has total freedom to put the cameras anywhere, but realistically will limit the positions the camera is to be set up. Particular care needs to be taken that shots will cut together – not always the case if the camera position is leaping wildly all over the place. Thought needs to be given to the practicality of each camera set-up – has the camera operator got room to achieve the shot? Remember that what probably takes the biggest element of time in PSC production is the set-up and strip-down time for the camera equipment.

The tendency for PSC is to spend less time rehearsing since each set-up only deals with one shot, and there is time for performers to run through their actions while the technical crew are setting up. What the Director does need to work out, though, is which performers are needed at which location and when. This often becomes quite a protracted period, and may be more difficult to cast for than a studio shoot which might all be over in a couple of days.

Planning the schedule is also considerably more complex than for a studio production. In studio the usual pattern is to book the whole set-up for a short, intensive period. On location the cost conscious Director will have an intricate schedule of exactly what equipment and which personnel are needed over a number of days. Time must be allowed for travel, set-up and strip-down and, importantly, for the schedule slipping due to, for instance, bad weather delays.

An additional responsibility of the Director which pulls together a number of the above processes is to go and recce all the locations, making detailed plans about how they are going to be used.

The PA still has to assist with all the admin work of setting up a programme, but additionally he will have to arrange for permissions to be acquired for all the intended locations, arrange transport, catering and perhaps accommodation for everyone involved, and book equipment.

In production

On an actual shoot the way both Director and PA operate is very different from in studio. They are no longer in a separate area from the action, so they cannot speak during the takes (or the microphones will pick them up). The Director will give detailed instructions before the recording starts to all the crew and performers, perhaps trying a couple of dummy runs before going to record. She must ensure that each shot has sufficient overlap at beginning and end to allow for later editing, and must get plenty of cutaways. Often a Director may shoot the same sequence from different angles, and with different shot sizes to allow for decisions to be made at the edit.

The PA will not be concerned with script reading and warning, since each shot is relatively short everyone will know exactly where they are in it. Similarly there is a lot less need for timing to be precisely adhered to at this stage. Often the timing can be manipulated at the edit, removing the need to get it exact at the shoot.

Two areas of the PA's duties become much more significant. Firstly everything that is recorded must be accurately logged. This saves enormous amounts of time at the edit stage, and therefore lots of money!

Secondly the continuity of action must be scrupulously recorded and corrected. Any errors may lead to impossibility of cutting and again much expense.

Post-production

At the edit stage the Director is obviously still intimately involved in decision making, choosing which shot to cut to, how to layer up the sounds and so on. The PA will be of great help by referring to shooting logs ensuring that the minimum of time is wasted searching for the required shots.

The whole editing and post-production process is covered in more detail towards the end of the book.

15 Location lighting

Location lighting must be easy – you've got all that natural light there already! Nothing could be further from the truth. In fact location lighting is so difficult it's almost impossible, but don't give up yet! The two main problems are too much light and too few lighting tools. They need to be addressed together, but to understand them better and move toward solutions it might be a good idea to treat them separately.

The problem of too much light centres round the fact that natural light is not where you most need it to get the best shot. Daylight is the usual culprit, and one of the main difficulties with daylight is that it changes. Even taking out the obvious that there is less light at night, during the course of a day the quantity and colour temperature of daylight is constantly changing – especially if the weather happens to vary between cloudy and sunny. This change may be anything from unnoticeable to inspiring, for people watching with their naked eyes, but to a Lighting Supervisor, trying to get consistent shots, possible to edit together despite having been shot at different times, it is a nightmare.

Controlling daylight

How then might we start to control the impossible? The first decision point is indoors or outdoors? Indoors, daylight can be suppressed if not completely removed. At the very least it should be possible to remove the difference between sunshine and cloud. Sunshine gives hard shadows, which if they're not in the right position for the shot will be intrusive. Closing venetian blinds, drawing curtains, even just putting paper or some diffusing material over direct windows will help to bring the shadows under control. The daylight then provides a soft illumination which just could (with luck) add to a portable light and control its contrast.

Soft or hard, cloudy or sunny, daylight indoors tends to come in large quantities, and come in horizontally, so if you can't remove it, it is probably a good idea to try to align the camera and subject so that the light direction is helpful rather than intrusive. Unfortunately that decision is down to the director (and maybe the camera operator) rather than the Lighting Supervisor.

If you are outdoors then the assumption must be that the director wants some effect of daylight. In a sense this makes it easier for the Lighting Supervisor since the main lighting plot is provided, but in reality the uncontrollability of daylight is still a problem. The real difficulty is to be able to provide matched shots from different lighting. Being aware of weather conditions, time of sunrise and sunset, and which way is east (and of course the other compass points) will help the Lighting Supervisor to predict how the grander lighting plan of nature is going to affect theirs.

It is almost impossible on outdoor locations to suppress the effect of daylight, but sometimes, by judicious supplementing, it is possible to take advantage of natural light. A carefully placed soft light, for instance, may help to lift the shading caused by the sun on a performer's face, and allow it (the sun) to be used as a key light. Because natural daylight is plentiful, however, supplementing it tends to be done only by big wealthy productions, which can afford generators and large luminaires.

What tools can be used?

Unlike the studio where there may be a generous grid full of luminaires, and the flexibility of a powerful dimmer system to control them, the Lighting Supervisor on location has to try and deliver well-lit images using lights that can be carried in a suitcase. Perhaps this is counterbalanced by the fact that there will almost always be a fair quantity of ambient light which can provide the basic illumination, so the work of the Lighting Supervisor is more to do with interpretation.

Location lighting must be portable, by definition. This means that the luminaires are small and robust. A very common unit is the 'redhead' – an open-faced spotlight with a simple reflector and movable lamp. The body of it is made from glass-reinforced plastic, which both absorbs the knocks of frequent installation and strip down, and remains cool to the touch when the luminaire has been on for a while. By altering the position of the lamp the spread of the beam can be changed from spot to flood. It should be remembered though that putting the luminaire to flood does not make it soft.

There is a very simple reason why portable lighting units tend to give hard light rather than soft. Soft lights have to be big, therefore they are not very portable. Hard light can be softened though, either by putting a diffuser in front of the luminaire or by bouncing the light off a large white (or reflective) surface (such as a ceiling).

Controlling the amount of light is tricky. The simplest way to reduce quantity is to move the luminaire further away from the subject, but some finesse is needed in the choice of luminaire position. Simply banging the luminaire straight onto the action may produce excessive brightness (apart from the ugly shadows). Careful change of the spot/flood control, which alters the density of light within the beam may help to bring down a highlight. Similarly judicious realignment of the beam so that the action is not quite in the centre may help to reduce unwanted brightness. Who cares if the brightest part of the beam is shining where the camera isn't looking? If neither of these bring the brightness down the Lighting Supervisor may have to use wire scrims in front of the luminaire, or even sheets of neutral density filter.

Battery powered lighting is available, which gives the Lighting Supervisor independence from the mains, but because it takes a fairly large amount of current it tends to be used only with small-scale shots (a close up of the interviewer for instance). Battery powered lights which clip on to the top of the camera, and take power from a battery on the camera give the camera operator total mobility, but can have unattractive effects on the background if the camera moves, as the bright hot spot traverses across the scene.

Whatever lighting source is used the Lighting Supervisor will need to give thought to the colour balance of the shots. If there is daylight as well as artificial light which one will be the colour used? If daylight then correction filters will need to be used on the luminaires. If the luminaires set the colour, then the invasive daylight must be corrected.

Lighting safety

There is a serious safety problem to be addressed with location lighting. Necessarily there has to be a fairly powerful light source which will both give out a lot of heat and take a lot of electrical current. Additionally it will need to be at quite a height off the ground, perhaps only supported by a stand which also has to be portable, so is less than sturdy.

The heat aspect can be taken care of by making sure that the luminaire is not physically close to anything. Remember that radiant heat performs pretty much like light, so if it's shining on it, it's heating it. Remember too that luminaires have slots and gaps in their bodies to allow heat to disperse safely, so don't obstruct them!

The electrical current problem is dealt with by ensuring that the luminaires don't overstretch the available power of the sockets that are supplying them. Spread the load between a number of sockets. Also ensure that your cables safely deliver the power but don't cause a hazard. They should never be left in a coil (which actually increases the heat within the cable!), should never be an untidy jumble, and should never be so tight that they lift up off the ground. Preferably they should be routed over doors or walkways rather than across them at ground level. They should always be taped, or otherwise secured to avoid tripping hazards.

The height problem is dealt with in lots of different ways, depending on how the luminaire is mounted. If it is on a tripod stand, the legs should be as wide as possible, without blocking walkways. The top of the stand should be tied, or taped to prevent movement.

16 The location camera team

As with all other aspects, the camera team on location is considerably smaller (and more mobile) than their studio counterparts, but once again their role is guided by similar principles. They are still aiming to give the director good, well focused, well-framed images that will tell the story, but now they have the extra responsibility of ensuring that the exposure and colour balance of those images is well adjusted. They also have the job of setting up the whole apparatus. A studio Camera Operator walks up to it and starts getting shots – a location one has to first unpack it, put it on a tripod, power it up, and adjust its iris, white/black balance before she or he can even think about shots.

So let's go through the process and examine the stages:

Unpacking the camera and putting it on a tripod sounds very simple, but a huge amount of thought will go into this, much of it from the Camera Operator. The director, on recce, may have come up with some ideas about where to place their camera positions, but often enough they will have only the vaguest of ideas about where exactly to get the shots from.

The Camera Operator must weigh up what image the director needs against the practical considerations of each possible camera placement. Can they actually see the action from there? Is there anything which blocks the line of sight, is there sufficient space for the camera (and tripod) and its Operator, especially if movement is involved? What is happening in the background of the shot? Where will the sun cast shadows (if it should come out during the shot)? All these and more questions will be going through the Camera Operator's mind as she sets up.

What is the camera on?

What holds the camera up is another area of many questions. The director will have specified what nature of movement (if any) the camera must make in this shot. At its simplest there will be a camera looking from the normal height at a static scene. This requires the tripod to be set up and the camera firmly mounted onto it. The tripod provides a stable base for the camera, but it must be solidly positioned.

Not always, maybe not often, will the shoot be on firm level ground. Funnily enough here the tripod is the Camera Operator's biggest aid. It is impossible for a three legged device to rock (like a chair or table) if all legs are firmly on a surface. The fact that tripod legs can be extended to different lengths will also help to keep it level. Some tripods allow the whole panning head to move on the tripod legs, to achieve a level plane for the camera to rest on. This level is very important, because otherwise known verticals and horizontals in the image (buildings, water surfaces etc.) will look tilted.

If the camera has to move to follow action life becomes a whole lot more complicated. A simple dolly, or wheeled spreader on the bottom of the tripod legs may give some mobility on a smooth floor. Much more expensive (and therefore less common on small-scale productions) is the use of tracking. This is a specially laid mini railway line on which the camera (together with its tripod and Operator) can move smoothly.

For very mobile shots the Camera Operator may have to do without the benefit of additional support altogether. Professional cameras are designed to be used mounted on the Operator's shoulder. This uses the bone structure of the human skeleton to provide a (reasonably) stable support. In the control of an experienced (and fit) Camera Operator a shoulder mounted camera can be very nimble, but it fails when longer movements are needed.

The human action of walking (or running) is inherently unstable because of the alternate up and down movements caused by leg and foot movement. If this is necessary for following action the Camera Operator has another tool to call upon – the Steadicam. This is a system worn by the Camera Operator which smooths out any sudden movement. It is remarkable how smooth shots from it can be, but it is not weightless, so whereas an ordinary location Camera Operator has to be fit, a Steadicam Operator has to be super-fit! Steadicam is a registered trademark of the company producing this device which apart from being heavy and cumbersome is expensive. An increasingly common option is digital image stabilization. This is a system built in to many camcorders which helps to control camera shake and makes hand-held shots more acceptable. The system that controls the image stabilization is digital and is not connected with the recording system which may be Hi8 or S-VHS.

Power!

The power for the camera is probably the next problem to be dealt with. Most PSC type cameras work on a 12 volt DC supply. This can come either from internal batteries, or from an external supply. The latter can be either from a battery belt worn around the Camera Operator's waist, or if mains power is available nearby from an adaptor unit. Some cameras allow for powering from the VCR and this is an option which is worth using since the connection that provides the power also allows switching functions and warning lights about the VCR to be used at the camera. Unless on mains power the Camera Operator should be aware of the finite life of batteries. It is important to remember that the camera will use power whether or not you are recording the shot, so be aware of the total time it is switched on. Remember also that motorized zooms, irises and especially clip-on lights are expensive users of battery power, so be frugal in your use of them.

Adjusting exposure

Adjusting the iris of the camera is the next new problem for the Operator used only to studio work. The camera has a pick-up device (tube or CCD) which has a fixed sensitivity. To give good images it must be given the right amount of light. Too much light and highlights burn out while dark areas get pushed into blackness by the camera's protective electronics. Too little and colours lose their vividness, and tonal range is compressed. To control this, and ensure good exposure, a variable size hole at the back of the lens – the iris – is adjusted. On location this is done by the Camera Operator.

Luckily the effect of iris adjustment can be seen immediately on the camera viewfinder, or on a monitor fed by the camera. Burnt-out textureless highlights, with severe dark areas, need a smaller iris (with bigger 'f' number). Muddy colours, no true white or black areas (assuming the camera can see such tones) need a larger iris (with smaller 'f' number). The Camera Operator can find the correct exposure by gently rocking the iris control back and forth in smaller amounts on either side of good exposure, until the one and only accurate setting is found.

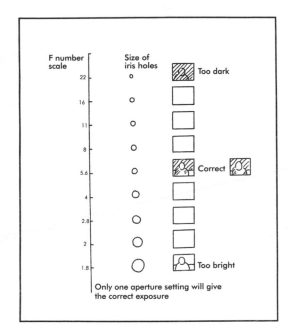

Figure 16.1   Scale of f number against size of iris hole against lighter and darker pictures

Apart from the simple requirement of getting correct exposure they will also have to think about what is important to see in a shot. For example, a person sitting in front of a window will cause problems of exposure. Exposure for the part of the image the camera sees through the window will leave the face in dark silhouette – obviously wrong. More often than not the actual brightnesses of different areas in a location shot are well in excess of the contrast range the camera can deal with, so a decision has to be made which part of the image is correctly exposed. Automatic irises can sometimes help, but they will fluctuate with any change in the scene, so are not preferred.

Colour balancing

The final adjustment the location Camera Operator has to make before they can get on with composing shots is the colour balance of the camera. Our eyes are intelligent and automatically read the correct colour of what we

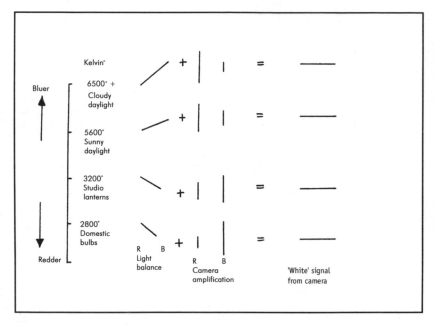

Figure 16.2   To correct the camera's rendition of a known colour (white) under lighting with a colour cast, its amplification of the red and blue signals is adjusted. The colour of the light on the scene is measured in degrees Kelvin

see in a wide range of lighting conditions. Unfortunately the camera is not, and will show accurately what it sees. There is a coloration to all light, so that a white piece of paper will look blueish under cloudy daylight, but quite red under ordinary domestic lighting, or production lights. The Camera Operator has to tell the camera which colour of light it is working in so that it can still render the white paper as white. This process is done at both ends of the tonal range – white and black – and is called white balancing and black balancing.

For the white balance it usually happens in two stages. The first coarse one is achieved by placing a corrective coloured glass disc between the lens and the pickup. This is part of the camera's optical system, and can be selected by turning a small wheel near the back of the lens. Usually there will be a listing printed on the camera near this control. It may have symbols or numbers to signify which disc to use. The numbers are the scale by which the colour cast of light is measured, or the colour temperature scale. On this scale higher numbers signify bluer light. Daylight could be anything from about 5600 degrees Kelvin up to over 10,000. Studio lighting and portable 'tungsten' type lighting is about 3,200 degrees K, whilst ordinary domestic lighting drops down to about 2,000.

Once the first adjustment is made the Camera Operator has to frame up a correctly exposed shot of a known white subject (a white card or sheet of paper will do) under the lighting that is to be used in the shot. It is important that this white source is in the area where the main interest of the shot is (in front of the performer's face is a good place to hold the card), not somewhere with perhaps a slightly different lighting balance, and certainly not right in front of the camera lens. With this shot set up the Camera Operator then initiates an electronic white balance procedure in the camera. This makes the camera remove any part of the signal which is not white by altering the amount of electronic amplification it gives to the red and blue signals. The green signal remains unchanged, which means that lighting which casts a green colour (such as fluorescent lighting) cannot be corrected for.

Some cameras have automatic white balance setting, but like automatic irises these can sometimes be troublesome, as they will change visibly as a shot develops.

The black balance is also set electronically, but it can do so without any lighting or shot requirement. Either the iris automatically shuts down as part of the procedure, or the lens cap can be put on to give the camera an image which is defined as black. Once again the red and blue signals are balanced to remove any other coloration.

Often cameras have memories which retain white and black balance settings. This can save a little time if you are going back to a known and predictable lighting set up, but more often you will have to do the balances anew for each new shot.

Shots at last!

Now with all these set-up arrangements done the Camera Operator can get on with the interesting part of the job – getting good images. Of course the same composing rules and movement rules as used in studio apply, but there are two additional things the location Camera Operator needs to consider.

Firstly they may very well be in control of VCR functions (especially if using a camcorder) so they will have to initiate recording.

Secondly, the director and editor will need plenty of choice about what to cut together at the edit stage, so a good location Camera Operator will always be on the lookout for good cutaways (buffer shots to go between otherwise uncuttable joins) and recording them, without the need to be asked.

17 The location sound team

The make up of the location sound team is led by demand. Obviously someone must be responsible for sound, but how big is the team?

It is possible with modern camcorder equipment to make the sound person the equipment itself. All you need is a microphone built into the camcorder, some form of automatic control over the recording level and sound, of sorts, will be recorded in synchronization with the pictures. Anybody who has tried their hand at the 'and the camcorder came too' type of holiday will recognize the simplicity of this system. They will also realize the disappointment it can cause.

It is equally possible to take a portable mixing desk, a range of outboard equipment, several microphones, boom operators, timecode generators and portable DAT tape recorders to recreate a situation as close to a studio environment as you will ever see.

It is really a question of what is required in the way of location sound, and what can be added later, that will dictate the make up of the sound team.

What do we need to record?

First of all, a quick reminder of the difference between studio and location recording. In the closed environment of a studio, with a crew of many people, we have all the facilities needed to put together a linear programme.

It is recorded complete, as it happens, with minimal editing. This means that the sound will effectively be a live mix of the programme. Any music or sound effects are normally mixed with the dialogue as we go along.

On location we shoot out of order, with a minimal crew, and then carefully edit everything together to form the linear programme. It is at the editing stage that we will add the computer graphics, the titles and all the visual transitions. Once the picture track has been finished there is really no reason why the audio can't be mixed, edited and added too if necessary. This stage is called post production which we will look at in more detail later.

There are only two types of sound that need to be recorded on location. A Sound Supervisor might sum it up by saying 'Get me good, clean sync sound and lots of buzz track.'

Sync sound

Sync sound (synchronous sound) needs a little explanation because it is all too easy to imagine it as simply dialogue, the actual words that the performers speak. In reality it is all the sounds that need to be in synchronization with the picture, as seen by the viewer. Take as an example two people in very long shot coming over a hill and talking. The visual effect is good, but what about the sound? The chances of us being able to see their lips moving on a small screen is so remote as to be discounted. The conversation could be added as a voiceover later. There is no need for sync sound. On the other hand if a glass of wine is being poured at a table, we would notice if the wine flowed into the glass and then the sound of it was heard, and continued after the wine had stopped being poured. Here there is a need to record the actual pouring as sync sound.

Buzz track

A very important thing to remember about audiovisual experiences, such as television or film, is that these audio and visual experiences must be complementary – they must work together. We need audio 'clues' to complete the picture. In our previous wine pouring example it would be fair to ask 'where are we?' If the camera zooms out to reveal a restaurant in total silence, I wouldn't want to eat there! We need some atmosphere. It is this general background buzz that gives its name to 'buzz track'.

Depending on where, and with whom, you are working you will also find that buzz is called 'atmos' (atmosphere) or 'ambient'. What you actually call it does not matter as long as you get lots of it! The visual equivalent is the 'cutaway', something that can be added later to help get over an awkward edit or, in the case of sound, can cover up a difference in background levels as the camera angle is changed. Buzz gives a sense of continuation between two shots that may have been recorded at very different times with very different actual levels of background sound. The continuing unbroken buzz added behind them at the edit stage deludes the viewer into thinking they actually took place in the same place and at the same time.

The idea of getting 'good, clean sync and lots of buzz' comes from the fact that it is easy to add sound later, it is almost impossible to take it out once mixed together. If we could separate the sync sound at the recording stage, we could add the right amount of buzz later. Not doing this causes the 'holiday camcorder' problem of everything being mixed together in the wrong proportions.

There are three ways of recording buzz. One is to wait until the actual recording has stopped, and then ask for quiet on the set whilst a sound only recording is made of the background. This will work, but you will only get a recording for as long as the director and rest of the crew, who want to pack up and move on, will allow.

The second alternative is that there is usually more than one audio track available on the video recorder. If sync is being recorded on one track, why not fix up another microphone to record buzz on another track? The position of this microphone needs to be thought out because all we need is the general background, not a rather poor recording of the sync sound added to the background.

The third method is similar, the background we want is going to be used at low level to add to the sync sound to give an atmosphere. It could be recorded onto a separate audio cassette recorder whilst shooting is actually taking place. Again, thought is needed regarding the placing of the cassette recorder during shooting.

If all else fails, it may be possible for the sound crew to visit the location at a later date, much as the camera crew may to collect some 'pick-up shots'.

The real art in working in an uncontrolled environment is totally to separate the sync sound recording from the background noise. This will give the sound editor the opportunity to add just the right amount of background. The final mix needs to sound natural, with enough atmosphere to complement the pictures.

Microphones on location

All that was said earlier, when we looked at microphones in the studio, also applies here. We will only look at the different requirement for recording on location.

From the sound team's point of view there are two things that are going to cause problems on location. One is the higher level of background noise, the other is the probability of wind interference if the recording is outdoors.

The key to the first point is an understanding of sound itself. Sound waves are vibrations of air that move outwards from the source, like the ripples in a pond. These vibrations have the energy to push the air in front of them causing this 'ripple' effect. Eventually all the energy is absorbed by the air and there are no more vibrations. The sound can no longer be heard.

This is something we all know, but think of it as the further away from a sound we are, the quieter it is. If you are sitting at a noisy table and someone across the room speaks to you, you have difficulty in hearing them. There is more sound energy from the table, because it is closer, than from your friend because they are further away. You may get up and walk towards them, or they may shout to produce more sound energy. This is the clue as to where to place a microphone.

It may be very convenient to have a microphone fitted to the camera, but the sounds it will pick up best will depend on what it 'hears' as the loudest. The closer sounds of the camera operator's movements, breathing, or the crew and equipment will be louder than someone speaking perhaps three or four metres away. We will be concentrating on what is being said and may ignore what is actually being picked up by the microphone.

Whenever you are making recordings on location you must listen to the sound being recorded. There is no other way to judge it other than to wear headphones and listen to exactly what is being picked up.

From our understanding of sound it would be fair to ask 'why is the microphone three or four metres from the source?' What is needed is to place the microphone as close to the source as possible. Like studio the starting point to doing this is to ask whether the microphone can be seen in shot.

Microphones in shot

With a straightforward interview, or a vox pop (literally, 'the voice of the people', a collection of opinions from members of the public), this is no problem.

There are no magic answers to solve the problem of which type to use, but it is more normal to use a dynamic microphone than an electrostatic type, because of their ruggedness and better ability to withstand location work, and cardioid would be a sensible choice of polar response.

This requires the presenter to move the microphone between themselves and the guest who will, almost inevitably, speak at a different sound level. A good presenter will compensate for this by moving the microphone closer to the guest, to avoid the need for the sound operator to adjust the level with the consequent, unwanted, rise in ambient. Sometimes these are replaced by, or supplemented with, clip-on microphones. Using two microphones, recording onto different tracks of the video recorder, means that any balancing of levels can be done easily at the edit stage.

Microphones out of shot

When the microphone cannot be seen in shot, with drama or a moving presenter for example, we are back to concealed microphones or booms. Lightweight fishpoles are used much more often on location than in studio. The sensible choice of microphone would be a cardioid dynamic, but often more control over the directional response is needed to try to cut down the background noise. In this case a Super- or Hypercardioid would be used. These polar patterns are really cardioid but with less pick-up from the sides. Hypercardioids are the familiar 'rifle' microphones, so called because they look like a gun barrel.

Often rifle microphones are preferred because, whilst offering a narrower acceptance angle, they tend to be better at picking up acceptable levels of sound at greater distances. This might seem to be exactly what is needed but, as a way of understanding some of their problems, they can be compared to a telephoto lens. Like the telephoto lens the whole scene is compressed. The background seems closer and it is the sounds in the background that we don't want. For this reason the correct way of pointing a rifle microphone is such that it can 'see' the source we want, and no other source. This involves either using them at a high angle and pointing them downwards, so that the background is the ground, or, perhaps easier for the boom operator, low down and pointing upwards towards the source. This will give the sky as the background.

If a decision is made to conceal microphones on the performers, the normal choice would be small clip-on radio microphones with the microphone and transmitter concealed under clothing. Care needs to be taken that the microphone does not rub against the clothing, producing an unwanted rustling sound, and that the microphone is not so obscured from the source that the resulting sound is muddy and indistinct. These radio microphones are normally omni-directional. In a studio, radio microphones need to be quite high powered and the receiver is often some distance from the transmitter, involving complex aerial systems and outputs connected to a mixing desk. Location radio microphones will often have small battery operated receivers clipped to the camera, from where they can get their power, with a short lead direct to the camcorder or separate video recorder.

You must remember that if the choice is to use radio microphones they are radio transmitters. As such they will need a licence before they can be operated. Heavy fines, and confiscation, will result if any interference is caused to emergency service transmissions or, worse, hospital monitoring equipment. Wherever radio microphones are used on location, the owner of the property should be informed so that any potential problems can be dealt with before shooting commences. It is an odd fact of law that, whilst it may not be illegal to sell a product, it may well be illegal to use it!

Wind noise

To be obvious, wind is movement of air. Movement of air is picked up by the microphone and converted into sound. Just because we cannot hear it does not mean that it is not going to be recorded. You will only hear the effect if you are monitoring the recording using headphones as suggested earlier.

To minimize the effect of wind, we need to prevent it reaching the microphone. This might seem obvious, but to prevent this movement of air, caused by the wind, reaching the microphone must also mean that other movement of air, caused by the sound we want, is prevented from reaching the microphone as well.

A compromise must be struck. It may be sufficient to reposition the microphone so that it is not directly facing the wind, this may not be possible or as effective as we hoped. The alternative is either a cheap compromise or an expensive solution.

The cheap compromise is easily understood by thinking of what we do in winter. When the wind becomes very strong we cover our ears up with a scarf or a hat. This prevents the high pressure wind causing pain to our ears, but we can still hear. If you think about what we actually hear you will realize that covering our ears in this fashion has made the sound more muffled, most of the high frequencies have gone. The compromise is that, while our ears don't now hurt, we also don't hear the full natural sound. Similarly with a microphone, it is possible to cover it up. All manufacturers provide 'wind socks' for their microphones. These are inexpensive and very good for minimizing low levels of wind. They are often called 'pop' filters because their real job is to cut down on breath noises and, particularly, the explosive consonants like 'p' and 'b'. They are, however, next to useless with high levels of wind.

The expensive solution is to go to a special manufacturer who produces proper 'wind shields' designed to eliminate the higher winds. The solution is expensive because these special wind shields are what is known as 'acoustically transparent'. They are designed to allow sound through but, at the same time, dispersing the wind. There are two factors that make these wind shields expensive. One is the material used (often pure lamb's wool) and the other is the need to design carefully a structure which will break up the wind, and disperse it, at the same time as allowing the sound through. Normally the structure will be in the form of a basket which totally encloses the microphone. These can often be seen on the television news programmes during location news gathering.

If the basket is not sufficient on its own then it must be covered with the 'furry jacket'. These can often be seen on news programme street interviews. Of course these windshields can be fitted to microphones on fishpoles and kept out of shot for drama programmes.

Automatic level control

Almost all camcorders and separate video recorders will have a method of automatically adjusting the recording level. This may be called ALC (automatic level control), or AGC (automatic gain control). Ideally this should be switchable, allowing the choice of automatic or manual control.

Whether to rely on automatic recording level adjustment or not is a personal matter. Understanding how it works and the aural effect of automatic recordings will help you to make a decision.

Manual recordings are made by adjusting the recording level control until the loudest sound just comes up to the red on the recording meter. This is also marked 0db, and signifies the optimum recording level. At this level we get the best possible signal to noise ratio, the best balance between the maximum recording level before distortion and the minimum noise.

Any sounds that are quieter than this level are normally meant to be quieter, somebody whispering for example. With manual recordings we have the opportunity to make decisions about whether to adjust this quieter level and make it slightly louder or not.

In a music programme containing a great dynamic range, from loud to soft, we may be constantly making slight adjustments to the recording level. We are choosing to alter the dynamic range.

Automatic recordings are made by the machine. There are no recording level controls for us to adjust. We can no longer make decisions about the dynamic range that is being recorded. This might seem like an ideal situation. You are on sound today, you stick a microphone up somewhere and leave the rest to the machine. Perhaps you can get away with it altogether by saying 'let's use the microphone fitted to the camera.' Perhaps a little unprofessional?

Let's ask a couple of questions: 'How does the machine know what is the loudest sound? How does the machine know what is the quietest sound? The answers are simple – it doesn't. It can only guess and depending on the sophistication (expense) of the system in use it will be obvious, or very obvious, that a form of automatic recording is being used.

What the machine will do is accept the first sound to be recorded as being the loudest, if a louder sound comes along it will accept that as the loudest and adjust the level accordingly, next time we go back to the first (quieter sound) it will accept that as the loudest, and re-adjust the level, and so on. In other words it will try to balance all the sounds out so that they are all more or less the same level.

It depends on how expensive the system is, whether it can recognize that speech has pauses in it, and leaves the level set for that speech in the breath pauses or not. If not, the next sound it hears may be quite a high background sound, traffic perhaps, which is adjusted up to the level of the speech only to be pushed down again when the louder speech comes back. How long it allows before it compensates is crucial: too quickly and the sound will have a 'breathing' effect of speech, with quiet traffic in the background, followed by loud traffic, followed by speech with quiet traffic in the background again, and so on. If it is too slow, the effect will sound as if the following sound is being slowly faded up.

Automatic recording on most modern equipment works very well but, if the location crew has a sound operator and the equipment has the choice between manual or automatic recording, you will always get better results by controlling it manually.

18 A little more paperwork

The difference between location and studio

A location programme will still go through all the stages from conceptualization to scripts that were mentioned in the first section on 'a little paperwork', indeed one of the examples used was based on a location insert. Here we will only look at the additional paperwork that will need to be generated for a location shoot.

The studio is an enclosed environment, with all the cameras, lights and sound equipment already fitted, and the programme normally continues in a linear fashion using the vision mixer to 'edit' between the required shots. A location shoot is totally different, normally using only one camera to get all the shots which are then edited together later into a linear programme.

Portable single camera shooting (PSC) is much more like film shooting, where everything has to be taken to the location, erected, connected, dismantled and moved to the next location. In larger productions there will be an Assistant Director and Location Manager to look after the smooth running of the shoot, but in smaller productions the work normally falls to the PA.

The location

Once a location has been chosen, be it a park, a street, or inside an hotel, the first thing to do is to find out who owns it and who can give permission for it to be used. This will generate a very important piece of paper that goes into the 'permissions file'. This piece of paper may not be a contract, as such, but will be a letter from a named person actually authorizing you to be there, at a stipulated time, for the purposes of shooting that scene. There should be a local contact name and phone number of a person that can be contacted to verify this permission if a request is made. Obviously you need one of these 'permissions' for every location, hence the 'permissions file' that must be available at every location whilst the shooting takes place. Time is often wasted when a crew turns up at a location and, when challenged, can only say 'but the manager said it would be all right'.

The recce

Recce is the industry shorthand for reconnoitre. This involves thoroughly examining the location, drawing up plans and checking what facilities are available. Again this is often left to the PA, but it helps if the camera operator and an electrician can be present. The purpose of the recce is to find out what problems may occur whilst actually shooting at this location. The questions that need answering fall into two categories: physical and physiological. The physical questions that need answers should be drawn up as a scale plan. What is needed is a set of diagrams similar to the studio plans, but they must be created for each location. A few typical questions that will help provide the answers are: How big is the space? How high is the ceiling? Where are the doors/windows? What colour is the wall/ceiling? What is the available light? From where? How many power sockets are there? What sort are they and how much current is available? What obstructions are there (a large signpost or parking meters may need to be 'camouflaged' by a horse and cart in a period drama)? What access is available for people, vehicles and equipment? Particularly helpful to the sound team will be: What is the level of ambient noise? What type of noise (obvious disasters occur when nobody noticed the church clock which strikes on the quarter hour, or the fact that the room is immediately opposite the fire station)?

The physiological questions concern the well-being of the crew and performers. Again, examples would be: Is there somewhere discreet for performers to change/make-up? Where are the nearest toilets? Where is the nearest place for refreshments (or do you need to make arrangements for location catering)? Where is the nearest telephone? How do crew/ performers get to the location (draw them a map, or arrange transport)?

It is from these recce plans and notes that the director and crew can work out shots, camera positions, lighting positions and requirements, sound requirements and foresee any problems that may occur. With small-scale programmes notes and plans may be sufficient. For larger scale programmes, the notes and plans are often supplemented by photographs or actual video footage.

Insurance

The whole question of insurance has to be considered very carefully. There is a legal requirement for public liability and third party insurance and you should check exactly what this covers. Additionally questions that need to be asked under this section are typically: Are the crew covered? Are the performers covered (particularly if stunts are involved)? Can you claim if crew or performers fail to turn up due to sickness? Are you covered if a light accidentally sets fire to the curtains? Do you need to take out special insurance to protect against loss of time (and money) in the event of adverse weather? Is the equipment covered against loss or theft on location? Are the vehicles covered for business use?

Applicable to studio work as well, but particularly relevant to location is the consideration of consulting a specially qualified solicitor and a specialist insurance broker. With small-scale productions this will add considerably to the expense of the production and provided everything that could possibly be thought of has been covered it is unlikely that anything will go wrong. However, with larger scale productions covering many locations the chances of something untoward happening increase with each location.

Shooting script

The golden rule with single camera production is only to visit each location once. This might seem very simple but it involves breaking the programme script into a shooting script.

A shooting script details all the shots that are required at each location, no matter where they eventually end up in the programme. In other words the programme is shot in a totally non-linear fashion.

The starting point is to go through the script and pull out each shot that occurs at the same location. The next stage is to narrow these shots down to which shots take place at what time of day. This is further broken down into which shots at this location, and this time of day, use the same performers. We now have an efficient use of time and people. The right people can be gathered at the right location for the right amount of time.

The problems with shooting like this are the need for continuity. The action may take place over weeks, but the shooting takes a matter of hours. The PA will not only need to keep a very close watch on the accuracy of the obvious events like performers ageing, scars healing or 'daily' changes of clothing but also the less obvious, but often noticed by the viewer, like the time on the clock on the wall never being the same as the wristwatch that can be seen on a performer, or something in the background that should not be there, a blockbuster period drama film recently had a vapour trail from a jet move slowly across the sky!

Call sheets

As with studio, performers and crew need to be called to be at the shoot when required. The call sheet is a document that will detail who is required where and when on a particular day. There is no standard form this should take, you cannot go out and buy a pad of call sheets, but they tend to be daily sheets. Apart from the name of the production, the director and the date, the information needed is best thought of by answering a few questions: Who is to go? Where are they to go? How do they get there? What time are they required? Who is the named contact? Is there a contact phone number? What do they do when they get there? What time can they have a break (lunch for example)? What time do they leave? For crew call sheets there may be additional questions to be answered: Are there any technical requirements (special make-up, props, extra lights etc.)?

From these questions it is simple to see that it would help if the call sheet was broken into a 'diary' style document showing times against events, like arrive, shoot scenes 3, 52, 12, 9 and 6, lunch, leave. It may help to have a map showing how to get to the location and it certainly needs a point of contact should anything go wrong.

It may be that crew and performers are called to a daily production meeting early and then all go to the location together. If so this should be shown, but there is still a requirement for 'what is happening throughout the day' and a contact person and phone number.

Logs

Logs are an actual record of what was shot, in the precise order it was shot, with details of which shot it was and which take of that shot. They will also detail whether the take is usable and if so which part is usable.

There are two logs commonly used, one is the shooting log (a record of what was shot) the other is the edit log (a record of what should be edited to produce the final programme).

The PA should compile the shooting log actually on location as it occurs. It is a matter for individuals to decide its exact format but a typical one will have the name of the production, the director, the location, the date and, most important, the tape number at the top. This will be followed by five or more columns. Within the columns will be the shot number, a shot description, the take number, the start time of the take (this should be the actual timecode time if available or the real time from the start of the tape), the shot length, whether the take was usable or not (this is often shortened to OK or NG – no good). If a take is marked NG it helps to know why. NG Cam would mean that the picture is unusable, but the sound could be OK, NG Sound would mean the picture is usable but the sound isn't. Apart from these main columns many PAs will have a 'notes' column, for instance it may be that a shot that failed might contain a possible cutaway, or some possible ambient sound. Often when a director calls a cut a performer will relax and may provide a useful smile or a demonstrative movement which could be useful at the edit stage.

The second log is the edit log, which puts all the takes to be used in the linear order of the programme. From this list the editor will construct the programme so it is essential that it is accurate. Again it will be in columns and will detail the shot number from shot one to the end, which tape it is on, the exact start time on the tape, the exact duration and the type of transition to the next shot. It helps to have a shot description, but this isn't essential. If there is to be a 'split' edit, where sound continues under a new picture, or vice versa, this must be included. As we will see, this log is often produced by a computer at the off-line edit stage in the form of an edit decision list (EDL), which can be used actually to carry out the edits at the on-line stage.

Life becomes more complicated if non-linear editing is being used for the off-line stage, because if the edit log is not accurate, or timecode is not in use, it may be impossible to find a particular shot when on-line is done using the original tapes. Most non-linear systems will produce an EDL, but be warned there is no standard that will allow all on-line suites to understand all EDLs! An accurate edit log is the only answer.

Copyright

Copyright is really outside the scope of this book, but it must be said that everything from a piece of music, a photograph to a literary work belongs to someone. Anything, particularly music, used in a production, must only be used if you have the written permission of the owner. This may involve buying a licence. Obtaining a licence is always cheaper than the possible fine that will be incurred.

19 Editing

Perhaps the biggest advance in video production in the last few years has been in the editing process.

With the rapid fall in the cost of computer memory, the availability of larger hard disc storage space at affordable prices, faster processors and more advanced graphics cards computer editing is now much more accessible to the smaller video producer. This affordable access to computer technology has given rise to an upsurge in non-linear editing (NLE).

Editing is the process of putting the programme together. Studio productions are largely shot in sequence with all the effects and transitions incorporated. Minimal editing may be required to cut a programme to time, but the cost and complexity of studio work is such that you should aim to come out of a studio with the final programme. Titles, captions, inserts and effects are all under the control of the Director and Vision Mixer during production.

Single camera programmes, which involve shooting out of sequence at different locations, provide the source material that needs to be built into the originally intended programme.

Methods of editing

There are three distinctly different methods of editing programmes. The traditional method of 'cut and splice' where scenes are literally cut from the tape and stuck back in the correct sequence, as in film, has long disappeared but this idea of linear editing has remained and is still the most common method of editing. The drawbacks of linear editing lie in the need to copy the required bits of video and audio onto a new tape in the order required. Because the clips are in an order, and of finite time, any later change of mind about the length or position of a clip results in a new copy having to be made. In other words, a whole new edited tape has to be made from that edit point onwards.

Copying tapes produces a loss of quality which is why it is important that the acquisition is done on the highest possible quality, no matter what format you will eventually end up with. Often the original tape is copied to a digital format, edited with minimal loss of quality, and then copied back to the desired end format. This obviously involves the expense of digital machines and editing suites.

The second method of editing, based on the advances in affordable computer technology is non-linear editing (NLE). This method involves digitizing the source material and putting the files of material into a computer. The programme material can now be formed into a video programme using a computer editing programme. These programmes work exactly the same as a word processor (except that they process pictures and sound). Clips can be assembled into the right order using cut and paste techniques. Exactly like a word processor the clips can be added to, the order can be changed, bits can be taken out and so on. Editing can start on the day of the shoot or whenever there is enough material to make up sequences. NLE computer programmes will have a range of effects and transitions built into them doing away with the need for a separate vision mixer.

If you are using an NLE system it is very important that you keep to the discipline of programme making. A programme should be designed and constructed at the paperwork stage. NLE is a quicker, more flexible method of editing – it is not intended to be used as a tool for sloppy programme making whereby you can just go and shoot anything and then 'make' the programme using a computer.

The third type of editing is computer assisted editing (sometimes called hybrid editing). With this method a still frame (or sometimes a short clip) of the beginning and end of a scene is 'grabbed' by the computer together with its location on the original tape. This is normally the timecode number but, less accurately, can be derived from the control track. Each of these clips can then be cut and pasted into a storyboard displayed on the computer screen. Any transitions or effects between the scenes can be selected from the computer and added to the storyboard.

Because this method uses a computer programme to assemble the storyboard, and cut and paste is available, the order can be changed at any time during this assembly process. When the programme is complete the computer is instructed to make the final programme. It does this by copying the bits held on the source tapes in the right order, adding transitions as it goes, onto another tape.

This may be seen as the best of both worlds. It is possible to use the power of the computer to adjust and assemble the programme until it is the way you wanted it to be, and then use the computer to make the edited copy using the original source material rather than a sub-standard digitized version.

The editing team consists of few people – the Director and PA will, of course, be present together with the Editor. There may be a Tape Operator, Edit Assistant and/or sound person. With NLE the Director normally explains what is wanted to the Computer Operator who is an expert with the hardware and software and can find their way around them very quickly.

Whichever editing method is to be used, it is essential that you understand the basic concepts of editing. NLE uses these concepts, and the same terminology, and will be much easier to understand if you think of it as working with a picture and sound (word)processor having understood the basic concepts which are outlined here.

Off line or on line?

Editing is a very time-consuming process in its initial stages. The various clips have to be accurately located on the different source tapes, checked that they will visually join together and if not what can be done. Maybe a cutaway is needed, but whereabouts on which source tape is it? The PA's log will cut down a lot of time wasting if it has been done accurately, but checks still have to be made to see if the programme as a whole will flow as required. A 'rough cut' edit will often be required by the client before sanctioning a final version. Complicated mixes, transitions and sounds may need to be added.

Edit suite hire time is very expensive. Edit suites are not the place to log tapes, try out mixes or play with a series of ideas that may not work. Because of this editing is broken down into two stages, off line and on line.

Off line comes first and is carried out on the cheapest available system (time is money), it may mean copying all the source tapes to VHS which will both protect the valuable source tapes and provide the cheapest possible medium to work on. It is an essential that if the original tapes have been shot incorporating timecode this must be 'burnt' into the copies so that it is clearly visible on the screen. This BITC (pronounced 'bitsee') will form the basis of a list of all the required edits in the form of an edit decision list (EDL). An EDL is a list of all the locations for the first and last frame of each scene as they are to be joined together to form the final programme. An off-line edit is the rough cut edit. It will usually only have cuts between shots with, at best, a caption saying what sort of transition will be in the final version. The sound will be 'as recorded', and will not have been cleaned up or added to.

Only when you have a version of the off-line rough cut edit that everybody is happy with can you go to the next (most expensive) stage of on-line editing.

The on-line edit suite will have the ability to make the final programme from your original source tapes. Here the EDL will be fed to a computer which will control the machines and make sure they are at the right timecode point for each consecutive shot. Some off-line suites will even have codes that can be put into the EDL to be interpreted as a particular type of transition that will be carried out by the on-line suite. Beware if you are using this system as there are no standards laid down, different on-line suites will have different codes. A lot of time can be wasted in an off-line suite by feeding in effects and transition codes that cannot be understood by the on-line suite you have chosen.

Increasingly hybrid systems are being used which incorporate cheap, but poor quality, computerized non-linear editing (see later for an explanation of non linear) for the off-line suite and this will generate a rough cut version and an EDL for the on line suite.

The edit suite

What is the equipment used to edit? At its most simple editing can just about be done with a playback video machine, an edit record video machine, a monitor and some connecting cables, but this would allow little subtlety or control over the edits, so a very common package consists of five, maybe six units. There will be two video machines – one to play back raw material on, the other to record the final master tape on. The record one must be an edit capable one, which as well as doing ordinary

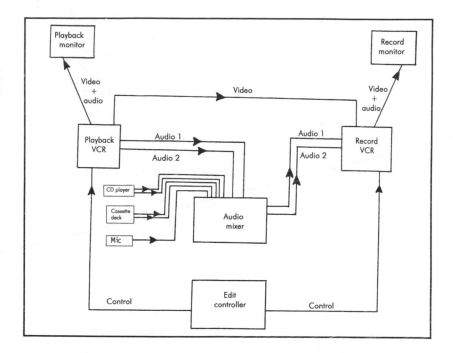

Figure 19.1 A schematic plan of a two-machine edit suite

recording has the ability to switch to incoming signals when editing. Each of these video machines will have a monitor to allow the Editor to see pictures and hear sound from them. It is possible to edit with just one monitor showing the output of the record machine, and then switching that to pass straight through its input signals, when it is necessary to look at the playback pictures, but this is obviously slower and less convenient than having two.

The edit controller allows both video machines to be controlled from one panel, and gives fine control abilities such as shuttle search. What it also does is automatically control all the editing processes, so that the machines will accurately edit at the Editor's chosen point. Many edit suites will also have a simple sound mixer to allow blending and balancing of sounds, and perhaps the addition of sound effects or music.

Tape editing: the basics

For simplicity of explanation we will assume that we have sound and pictures from a normal analogue video recorder rather than a digital recorder. Digital formats use the same principles of editing, often using the same type of edit suites as will be outlined here, but the original signals are made up of digital information which can be manipulated in different ways. It is possible to 'mix and match' so that normal analogue pictures can be treated to digital video effects (DVE) which give a much wider range of transitions and effects than the standard wipes or mixes available with the more basic equipment.

What is important at this introduction stage is that you understand the concepts of the editing process and don't get bogged down with the technicalities. You can be assured that whatever creative effects you want to incorporate into your programme are now possible. The cost and complexity of equipment is the only limit to your creativity! In the early stages of learning about video production, however, you are advised to master the basics and keep the programme as simple as possible.

When analogue sound is recorded onto tape it is stored as a series of magnetic pulses. These pulses of magnetism are analogous (copies of the original in another form) to the sound in terms of frequency and amplitude (volume). The video format you are editing the tape onto should allow you independent access to a minimum of two tracks dedicated to audio. We will see why this is necessary when we come to audio post-production.

Pictures, being a considerably more complex signal, require a more complex method of recording. Different countries have evolved different standards for encoding the picture which involves using a different number of lines of information for each new image (or frame) and a different number of frames in one second. The three main standards you will hear of are PAL (largely European and parts of the Far East), SECAM (France and parts of the Middle East), and NTSC (the USA and Japan). The good news is that you do not need to be concerned with the technicality of how it all happens – the bad news is that you must remember that standards are not interchangeable. A tape shot in the USA, for example, cannot necessarily

Figure 19.2   Magnetic pulses (like audio) on tape

be played back or edited on UK or French equipment. Increasingly manufacturers are producing 'multi standard' televisions and video players which will allow playback of different systems, but even these sets cannot be used to change the signal from one system to another.

An obvious, but often overlooked fact, is that the camcorder or video recorder is designed to record using a particular system. If you have a camcorder that records in PAL, for example, it will still record in PAL wherever in the world you use it. There may be problems with the mains voltage in use, but the recording system is dictated by the recorder, not the part of the world in which it is used.

The picture is still recorded as a series of magnetic pulses, but in order to record the structure of the picture in terms of brightness and colour of the frames the mechanism for recording has to allow for enormous density of storage. Technology is developing rapidly in this realm, with direct to disc, magneto-optical and virtual memory systems ready to take over, but here we are concerned with the fact that most video pictures are recorded by a head at the edge of a rapidly-rotating disc recording diagonally onto a magnetic cassette.

The process still lays down a series of magnetic pulses (that is the fundamental nature of magnetic recording), but these pulses are now extremely fine, and packed extremely close together, along a (relatively) long strip.

It is the limitations, and possibilities, of this recording process which set the technical rules for editing.

What we need to do is to start recording at a very precise place in the sequence of pictures. This will give the effect of a cut when it plays back, as the moment of recording start will be an apparent switch of image to the new one. What actually happens is the editing video recorder, on which the master tape is being compiled, switches into record mode in the gap between two consecutive picture frames. However this has a technical problem. Because the spinning disc must be at a very accurately controlled speed (as must the tape movement through the machine) for stable pictures to be recorded it is not possible for the recording video machine to start up instantly. What it has to do is go back to a point some distance before the chosen edit point and run up to it in the play mode, allowing speeds to settle and signals to lock up. This period in play is called the pre-roll.

Another crucial requirement is that the recording machine switches into record at the right point in the sequence of signals that represents picture frames being built, cleared off and replaced. If it switched, for

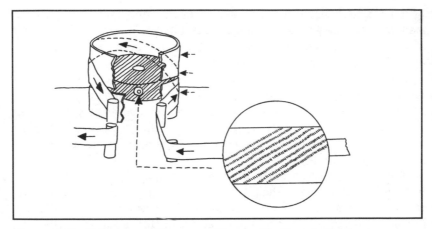

Figure 19.3   Helical scan video tape, with magnification of video track

instance, as one frame was only half complete, there would be an unpleasant flash on playback, and there may well be instability of some of the subsequent frames as the playback machine attempted to relock. The switch over to record must be in what is called 'vertical blanking' and it must be at the right point in the colour instructions cycle. So that the record machine can do this accurately it has to have some way of recognizing the structure of the last few frames before the edit point, to be able to match the structure of the incoming new frames to them. If this works, then on playback the structure sequence of the shots before and after the edit would appear to be an unbroken stream, and hence the pictures on the monitor would be stable and clean (despite changing to a new image at the edit). The way the machines do this is to record (when the pictures are first recorded) a separate signal, onto a separate track on the tape, which acts like a time reference pulse. This is called the control track.

So we can see that we have at least four separate signals, recorded on four separate tracks on the tape. These are the two sound tracks, the long diagonal picture track, and the control track.

What happens in an edit?

Let us assume we have dropped in on our Editor, just as she completes an edit. We will look at the details of how she sets up and executes the next edit.

The first stage is to find and mark the edit points. This can be done on either machine first, but for this edit she does it first on the record machine. We notice that there are tapes loaded in both the record and playback machines. To find the first edit point on the record machine the Editor presses the play button for that machine on the controller. She watches carefully (and listens) to find the exact moment when she wants to cut to a different shot. Actually she overshoots it slightly, so very carefully uses the shuttle control to wind the tape back to the chosen point.

The pictures on the monitor during this shuttle will have noise (or interference) on them, but this will disappear when the tape plays again at its correct speed. The numbers on the control panel, which were steadily going up when the tape was playing are now slowly going back down.

Once the point has been found the shuttle control is centred and the tape pauses, giving a still picture on the screen. The Editor now enters this point into the controller's memory (usually by pressing 'in entry' buttons).

The controller actually stores the number from the display, and you will realize these numbers are very important. They derive from the control track on the tape, as it plays, and the controller does all its automatic functions by counting these numbers backwards and forwards, and switching machine functions at the appropriate points. Any break in the control track (and therefore any break in the continuity of the numbers) will be fatal for the accuracy and stability of the edits.

The Editor now finds an edit point for the playback machine in exactly the same way. This point in the material will directly follow the point chosen on the record machine, when the edit is done. She may also wish to put in a third edit point which will specify when the edit ends. This could

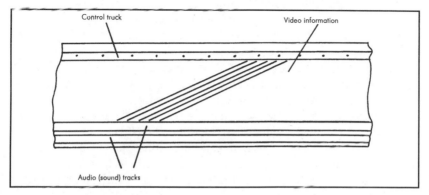

Figure 19.4   Different tracks on video tape

be from the playback machine (if for instance there is some material that must not be included in the edit, after the wanted shot had finished) or from the record machine if the edit was being put into the middle of pre-existing material. In either case it will determine the length of the edit. (Obviously you can't have out points on both machines!) Quite often though, when building a programme from new, there is no need to mark the end of the edit tightly. It can be allowed to over run slightly at the end, and then the following edit will crop any excess off the shot. This allows the Editor more freedom in the timing of the next edit.

Once the edit points have been entered the Editor will try a 'preview' of the edit. This shows what it will look like (and what it will sound like) on the monitor of the record video machine, without actually committing it to tape.

What happens is that both video machines will automatically shuttle back to a specified distance before the edit in points, (usually 5 seconds). Briefly they pause there and then roll forward in ordinary playback mode. At the edit points the monitor of the record machine switches to show the incoming picture and sound from the playback machine. At the end of the edit (if the Editor has specified an out point) the record machine monitor will drop back to playback of what is already on the tape. If the editor didn't specify an out point she will have to abort the preview when she has seen enough to judge whether it will succeed. Usually it is the beginning of the edit, where it joins onto the previous shot, that is critical, so the Editor probably won't need to go far beyond it to decide.

If it isn't quite right it can still be altered, and nothing has been damaged. Edit points can be moved, or sound levels adjusted. On complex, or very tightly timed edits, it may be necessary to run a number of previews before the Editor is satisfied with it.

Now the moment of truth – if all is well with the preview the Editor will press the 'auto-edit' button and this time the edit is recorded. Once more the machines roll back the pre-roll distance, pause and play forward, but this time the record is actually laying the new material onto tape. If you are going on to an empty tape, then there is no loss if the edit isn't right – it can easily be done again, but if you are editing into the middle of existing material the edit will record over the old material, so if it is wrong you cannot recover it. Be sure, on the basis of previews, that the edit is exactly right before you commit it.

The Editor will now check that the recording of the edit has taken place, and looks and sounds just as it should, by playing it back off the record machine or 'reviewing' it. If it isn't quite right it is much easier to redo the edit now, with everything still approximately cued up, rather than later when many other edits could have followed after it, and may have to be redone.

Two different types of edit

We saw earlier how the edit record video machine (together with the edit controller) ensures that the edit will play back stably and without interference by arranging to switch to record (from play) in the gap between frames. For it to be able to do this efficiently it must have technically stable (though not necessarily aesthetically good!) pictures presented to it before and during the edit. These will be coming from the source (or playback) machine, so that must be playing stably for the whole pre-roll and the whole duration of the edit. It must also have stable pictures on its own (master) tape during the pre-roll, to give a structure pattern to lock up to. These stable pictures imply totally stable control track signals before, at and during the edit, on both machines. Indeed if there are gaps in the control track, or it is damaged, the controller is unable to execute the edit accurately.

However, the record machine can be set to react in two different and distinct ways to the control track at the edit, and this gives the Editor a choice of two different modes of edit. These are called 'Assemble' and 'Insert' edits. It is important to remember that the phrases are technical definitions, rather than production ones. You can still assemble your programme onto an empty master tape using 'Insert' edits.

How then are they different?

With 'Assemble' edits the record machine, when it reaches the edit 'in' point, switches to new control track, derived from the incoming picture. At the end of the edit, when the machine stops, the control track collapses. There will be a short length of tape after the edit which has been erased, but on which no signal has been recorded. When this is played back the gap in the control track causes the picture to break up and become unstable. This will be the case even if there are existing pictures already on the tape after the edit. The transition from the end of the edit to the pre-existing pictures can never be stable because of the 'hole' in the control track. There is also a small possibility that, if the machine does not accurately match the new control track to the old one immediately before the edit there will be instability there as well.

With 'Insert' edits the record machine does not derive new control track, but locks the incoming pictures to the existing control track already on tape. At the end of the edit it simply switches from record back to playback, but the control track continues, unbroken. This means that we can achieve a clean cut at the end of the edit, back to pre-existing pictures. Because the control track remains untouched by the edit, and runs continuously from before it, through it and on after it, it is inherently more stable than an assemble edit can be. This type of edit also allows the possibility to edit pictures and either, or both, of the two audio tracks separately, so programmes can be built up in layers.

How do we choose which to use, and what are the advantages and disadvantages of each?

Insert edit

'Insert' edits are more stable, can be done as separated picture and sound tracks, cut clean back to existing pictures at the end, and can be done (if necessary) again and again at the same point, with no loss of stability. These are obviously powerful advantages, so naturally they should be the preferred choice of the Editor.

The main disadvantage is the master tape must be prepared before the edit can start, by having a continuous control track (of at least some seconds longer than the programme, probably the whole tape) recorded on to it. This can be done by recording any stable, continuous picture (colour bars, black – from a camera with its lens capped – or even images). Some edit suites may have a 'black and burst' generator or 'sync pulse' generator which could be used as the source for it. Unfortunately it is not possible to record this track faster than real time, so a 20 minute programme will need about 22 minutes of time to pre-record the control track.

Assemble edit

'Assemble' edits really only have one advantage – that of speed of preparation. You only need to record a short amount of control track before your first edit, so if you have an unformatted tape you can start editing within about five minutes. However this is at the loss of guaranteed stability and the ability to layer up your programme, track by track. You cannot put material in the middle of existing sequences, because of the collapse at the end of the edit.

Some edits

Using the 'Insert' mode of editing it is possible to use some important techniques. Let us look at the example of a short programme involving a presenter doing an introduction, followed by an illustrative sequence with a descriptive voiceover, followed by a conversation with 'an expert'.

We have already explained the difference between sync and non-sync sound when we looked at the location sound team. At the edit stage it is important that the editor keeps the sync sound separate from the non-sync sounds on one of the audio tracks. Any ambient sound must be put onto a separate audio track. The reasons for this will become clear when we look at audio post-production. A good editor will be mindful of what will help the sound person when the final stages of audio post-production are carried out. Often a sound person will be here, at the edit stage, to help with decisions as to what is recorded on which audio track.

If this is a small production and the editor is also the Director and sound person it will help considerably to have a sound track chart, as with a picture log, to assist with 'what goes where' in terms of the audio.

The first sequence, the introduction, is straightforward. There will probably be long shots and medium shots of the presenter talking to camera. These must be put into the correct order, and edited with pictures and sound together. Hopefully the professional presenter will have made few mistakes, and allowed gaps for editing into between different sections.

This leads into the section which illustrates what the programme is about. Do we need to hear ambient sound of the activity, or is it just as effective mute? Does it have a distinctive separate sound which can be identified with a visual aspect, or is it continuous undiscriminated sound? If the former, that sound, like the presenter's voice earlier, will need to be edited with the picture to retain 'lip-sync'. If the latter, we can first build a working sequence of pictures – using video only inserts – then add to it a continuous piece of the sound as 'buzz track' – using audio only inserts – to give the impression that all the shots are continuous in time.

The presenter's voiceover may already exist (perhaps as part of the introduction) or may be recorded after the pictures have been edited to fit them exactly. Either way it will be put on using audio inserts on the second sound track.

In the conversation the 'expert' may have muddled his words, or spoken out of the logical order, so his contribution will need to be restructured to make sense. This may result in similar images being cut next to each other – which would look ugly, so once the word sequence has been put together video only inserts are used to put bridging cutaways over what would otherwise be jump cuts. Perhaps we might also need to add some more explanatory voiceover from the presenter as audio inserts.

Later, perhaps when the client sees the programme, they ask for one of the images to be changed – maybe a new model has replaced the one shown. This is easily achieved by going back and replacing the incorrect image with a video insert.

More elaborate editing

The editing we have looked at so far made the picture joins exclusively by cutting, because that's how the switch from playback to record plays out. It isn't possible to do a partial recording, leaving residual parts of the picture underneath in addition to the new picture – the video machine is either recording or not, and if it is, it totally obliterates anything already on the tape.

In real programmes, however, there may be times when we need, for example, a slow dissolve from one image to another. This cannot be achieved in the simple edit suite described above. To achieve it we need another source machine, whose image can be combined, in some kind of vision mixer, with the image from the first source machine. So instead of one source feeding to the record machine we have two or more, and with the vision mixer all kinds of combinations which use images from both simultaneously can be used.

We need to ensure that the two images we wish to mix together are on different tapes, since we will be mixing from one source machine's output to the other's. You cannot put one tape into two machines!

We also need an edit controller which will tell both source machines when to roll. The assumption is that we start with one, which runs for a time, then we make a transition to the second which continues to roll for the rest of the edit. This process is known as an A/B roll, with the first machine to roll being called A, the second B. Because the timing of the changeover needs to be specified as well as the start and finish times of the edit, programming such a controller is more complex than for simple editing.

We also need to plan, and maybe programme into the controller, the kind of transition we want to happen between the machines.

Remember, though, that although we can now have a mix between shots as part of an edit, the record video machine will still only be able to start (and finish) the edit as a cut. With no further apparatus we can alternate cuts (starts/finishes of edits) and mixes (or other effects). If we had the ability to edit accurately between two consecutive frames of a shot we could hide the cut at the edit's start.

A little about timecode

On ordinary cheaper edit suites, operating on control track, there is an accuracy of about plus/minus 5 frames. This is quite adequate for most purposes, but it means if we try to edit between two consecutive frames of a continuing shot there is the possibility of slippage which shows as a twitch in movements within the shot. This accuracy can't realistically be improved if the machine relies, to know where it is on the tape, on counting control track pulses.

Timecode can solve this problem by allowing totally frame-accurate editing. This is done by (as well as recording control track) giving each frame of the video a unique numerical code which is recorded on to a separate part of the tape at the same time as the picture. It is always possible then for the machine to go to a precise location on the tape, and therefore to edit that accurately.

If we have, for example, frames 1-12, we could arrange to edit in a mix between frame 9 and 10. On playback the frame sequence would still go 1, 2, 3, 4, 5, 6, 7, 8, 9, 10, 11, and so on. It would give exactly the same appearance as the original sequence without the edit. So now we can hide the cut-in at start, and cut-out at end, of edit and just have visible the mix. Without timecode we could end with an edit giving a sequence 1, 2, 3, 4, 5, 10, 11 or 1, 2, 3, 4, 5, 6, 7, 8, 9, 7, 8, 9, 10, 11. Either of these would have unacceptable twitches at the point of discontinuity.

Timecode is used as the basic control signal, together with a synchronizer, to allow us the opportunity to lock other video machines or audio-tape recorders to one master recorder, so synchronous sound can be stripped off the video, processed, and then put back completely in sync.

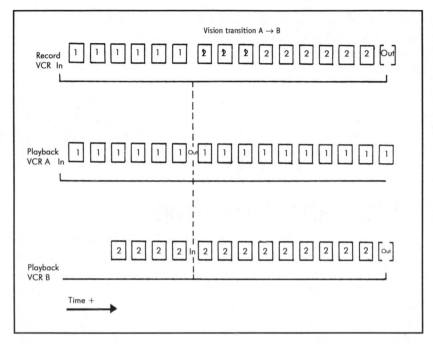

Figure 19.5   Time plan of edit points for a three-machine suite

The timecode from one of the various machines is designated as the master and read by the synchronizer. The timecode on the other machines (the slaves) is checked against the time of the master machine. The synchronizer now compares these times and sends out speed instructions that allow all the slave machines to run, in lock, to exactly the same time reference. The times do not need to be identical, but must be continuous, because it is possible to enter 'offsets' into the synchronizer. We might say 'the time on slave one is ten minutes behind the time on master' and the synchronizer will adjust to take this difference in 'timecode' time into account.

Timecode must be recorded as a continuous signal from one end of each tape to at least the end of the programme. When it is read back it displays the same figures as the control track (hours, minutes, seconds and frames), but they are the real time as recorded, not necessarily the time from the front of the tape. The actual timecode numbers are required by an EDL if the choice has been made to do timecode editing.

20 Audio post-production

Audio post-production is the final stage involved in putting our programme together. With so many different video formats, and the increasingly affordable option of non-linear editing, it is impossible to do more than look at the concepts involved in this 'basics' book. We will assume that the tape has come to audio post-production to have the audio track, which should be complementary to the picture track, cleaned up and finished off with music and/or effects and ambient sound.

We have been given the master tape which has all the sync audio on one track, leaving one other audio track for us to record onto. Hopefully, we also have an audio log to help find the bits of buzz track we will need from the various original video tapes and any audio tapes we made whilst on location. So where do we start?

The plan

The very least we are going to need to do is to add some music at the beginning and probably over the credits at the end. We may also need to add a voiceover or some sound effects. We may need to mix in some buzz track. We may need to 'clean up' the dialogue by adjusting the levels or using some equalization. We may need to add some reverberation or some other effect. What we need first is a plan showing exactly what we are going to do. To do this the Sound Editor will need to go through the whole tape and very carefully note down exactly what is needed at exactly what time. If timecode has been used life is easier, but if not an accurate time from the start of the tape will suffice.

The plan should end up looking similar to the picture EDL. It will be laid out in columns showing the time, what is needed and the duration. You will notice from CD sleeve notes about the times of tracks that punctuation marks are used to symbolize seconds and minutes. Seconds are shown as ", and minutes as ', so 2'47" is 2 mins 47 sec. We will use these in the example which might, for instance, have Time = 0", F/U (fade up) opening music (title, track number, how far in to the track it starts etc.), Duration = 15", Time = 15", F/O (fade out) music. Time = 1'16", raise level of voice by 4 dbs, Duration = 3" (it helps to have the actual words written down that need a level change). Time = 6'28", V/O (voice over) Duration = 18".

Simple post-production

With two independent audio tracks on the video recorder, it is possible to select which track we wish to record onto. If the sync sound is already on track 2, all we need to do is to select record on track 1 and record the music, voice over, buzz and effects in the right places onto track 1. If we now play back both tracks simultaneously this will give us a mixed sound track. Figure 20.1 shows this idea in pictorial form.

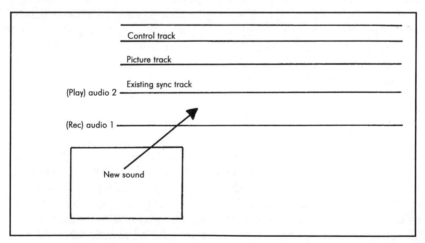

Figure 20.1   Existing sync sound on track two, new sound added to track one

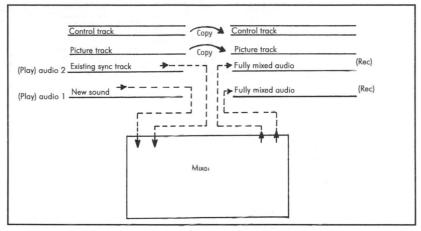

Figure 20.2   As Figure 20.1, but copied through mixer

What we haven't managed to do is to alter the quality or change the levels of the sync track. We could, however, make a copy of this master tape and make any adjustments we need, or add effects, by taking the audio tracks through a mixer. Figure 20.2 shows this idea.

The master tape remains intact and if we need to change the music or alter the levels at a later stage all we need to do is make the changes and then make another copy. What we have not ended up with is a fully mixed audio track on the master tape.

More complex post-production

The simplest way of getting a fully mixed audio track on the master uses a method known as Track Bouncing (also track collapse, or ping pong). This involves not only recording the music, voiceover, buzz and effects onto track 1, but taking the sync sound on track 2 out of the machine, sending it through a mixer channel and re-recording it onto track 1 at the same time. Everything is now mixed on track 1 and only the sync sound is left on track 2. All the facilities of the mixer are available during this re-recording so altering levels, adding equalization or reverberation are all possible. This is shown in Figure 20.3.

To free your hands, and brain, from the problem of cueing up new music and effects, if this can be done in the edit suite there is no reason why you

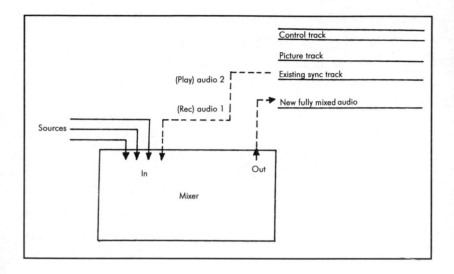

Figure 20.3   Schematic of sync being collapsed with new audio

shouldn't record the new music or effects onto a separate, blacked videotape which can be used in the player machine. Now it is a straightforward matter of setting up an 'audio only' edit. The music and effects will be available when you need it, it is only a question of adjusting the levels and equalization.

The ideal situation

The previous example of using the audio tracks of the player introduces the idea of creating a separate Music and Effects track (M&E). Using either the two tracks of a video tape recorder or, preferably, a multi-track audio recorder, it is possible to draw up a track chart. This will show the time position of the voiceover, music or effects in relation to the sync sound (take the beginning of the video as time zero) on each separate track. Each can now be recorded separately onto different tracks of the tape recorder. This makes overlapping, or multiple, sound effects very easy. You should record everything at the normal recording level, without fading in or out. This allows adjustments to be made to the mix when you compile the M&E and sync sound, through the mixer, onto the video recorder.

The real answer is to use timecode, a synchronizer and a digital multi track audio recorder. Over the last few years this option has become genuinely affordable for even the smallest of post-production suites.

Timecode (TC or SMPTE) is a recorded signal placed on both the video and the audio tapes which gives the exact time position on a tape in hours, minutes, seconds and frames. The synchronizer will compare the times it reads from both tape recorders and keep them both running together with absolute accuracy. The smaller, cassette based, digital audio recorders have a timecode and synchronizer board built in and do not need a separate track for the timecode, so all eight are available for audio. This concept is shown in Figure 20.4.

The possibilities with this system are endless. Because it is possible to run audio and video in absolute sync there is no reason why you can't take the sync sound off the video recorder, then make a complete multi-track audio mix before recording the complete mix back onto the video recorder in absolute sync.

Because you are using a multi-track recorder all the possibilities offered by track bouncing are available. You could end up with all the separate tracks fully mixed, with final levels, equalization, effects and fades all on one track ready to be re-recorded onto the video tape recorder.

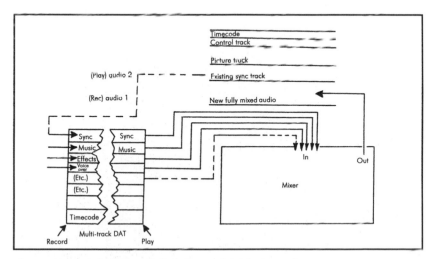

Figure 20.4 Schematic for digital 8 track with timecode

It is usual, and advised, to leave the sync sound on the video so that it can be used as a 'guide track'. This guide track can be played back whilst you record the new mixed audio onto the video recorder to allow you to compare the position of the original sync with the newly created audio.

Digital is now the firm favourite for even the small audio post-production suites. With computer prices falling and the ever increasing range of sequencer programmes it is possible to put together a very professional programme at truly affordable prices.

The current range of semi-professional non-linear editing programmes include a number of audio tracks that can be built up in much the same way as a multitrack audio recorder. Many have facilities built in similar to the audio sequencer programmes, whereby an 'audio studio' module is incorporated to perform the basic functions found in a normal audio mixing desk. The tracks can be assembled using computer files of MIDI or analogue sourced material, mixed, equalized and have effects added before outputting the finished audio to the final video tape.

21 The future

You, the new recruit to the video industry, are the future. It is you that will be the first to experience the massive explosion in new technology that is now beginning. Undoubtedly the future is digital. Digital technology should be viewed as two separate, and distinctly different, areas.

One area is the digital revolution in tiny chips that are, in effect, small computers. These already control image stabilization, extended zoom, exposure and light balance in modern cameras.

Bigger chips control video and sound capture, allowing the pictures and sounds to be manipulated within the digital domain of the computer. Digital video effects can be created by programmes that are specifically written to be incorporated in vision mixers and are also found within modules of non-linear editing programmes. Buying 'video capture cards' or 'non-linear editing programmes' often means buying a small computer contained within a plug-in card which is designed to be used in conjunction with a bigger computer which has storage space and an operating system. This is why these devices are known as 'add ons' or 'upgrades'.

The second area is that of digital recording. There is no mystery or complication to digital recording. If you remember the basics the worst thing is that you will have to learn a few more technical terms. The basic fact is that we have pictures we can see and sounds we can hear. These need to be stored somehow so that we can play them back when we want to. This book explained magnetic recording in a very simple way when we looked at editing, whereby these pictures and sounds are transferred into electrical signals which represent the pictures and sounds as analogue copies. These electrical signals are then transferred into magnetic signals, again analogue, which are stored onto a tape-based magnetizable material in the form of a handy-sized cassette.

Digital recording still starts with pictures we can see and sounds we can hear, they are still transferred into electrical signals but these signals are made up of a series of numbers, made up of noughts and ones, which represent the signal. Each nought or one is known as a bit because it is represented by BInary digiTS, the more bits used to represent a number the better. The minimum number of bits to represent one number is eight, eight bits are known as a byte. This will lead you to understand how we get 8-bit systems and that 16-bit systems are better (more bits per number) and you will probably have heard of 24-bit and 32-bit systems.

These bytes are stored as binary numbers by converting them to magnetic signals and recording them onto tape. The problem with digital video has never been with digital tape based systems. A digital edit suite, with tape based machines, works in exactly the same way as has been described earlier under 'editing'. Digital recording gives better quality pictures and sound and does not suffer from generation loss when copied.

The problem began when 'tapeless' systems were required. The massive number of bytes that needed to be stored meant that large amounts of memory were needed and memory costs money. The solution is to use some form of data reduction, known as video compression. The greater the compression, the greater the loss of quality. As an example, to compress six or seven minutes to the equivalent of S-VHS quality would require a storage space of around one gigabyte. The cost of disc drives is falling rapidly as is the ability to produce hard discs with massive storage space.

The next stage is to produce disc-based camcorders which will do away with the need to transfer the tape-based digital images to a computer memory. They do already exist but the need for storage space means that bigger capacity discs are needed than are presently available. The very forefront of technology now (end of 1998) is the Digital Versatile Disc (DVD), at the moment these are playback only but with a capacity of nearly 20 gigabytes and a better compression system than the current 'standard' this will soon become the next generation of storage systems.

It is a pity that the multi-format systems of analogue recording have been carried into the digital domain. Different manufacturers are leap-frogging over each other to provide the latest technology. The future will finally have arrived when all systems are equal and all interchangeable. It is strange that while it has been possible to buy an audio cassette recorder for the last thirty years that will operate happily anywhere in the world, with total interchangeability, the manufacturers have not taken the opportunity of the digital revolution to produce a compatible system.

Glossary

AGC — Automatic Gain Control. A circuit that automatically adjusts the recording level of video or audio signals.

AMBIENT SOUND — The background sounds within a scene (also atmos or buzz).

APERTURE — An adjustable hole in a lens through which the light passes. Used for controlling the amount of light.

ARTIFICIAL LIGHT — Any light that is not derived from daylight. Tungsten light has a colour temperature of 3200°K.

ASSEMBLE EDIT — Joining one scene to another using the existing sound, picture and control track.

ATMOS — The background sounds within a scene (also ambient or buzz).

AUDIO DUB — Copying or re-recording audio, without erasing the original track, or the video track.

AUXILIARIES — Additional outputs on a sound mixer. May be used to feed effects units or for foldback to the studio floor.

BACK LIGHT — A luminaire placed behind the performer to give depth, and separation from the background.

BARN DOORS — Metal flaps (like doors) in front of a luminaire to control the direction of the output.

BI-DIRECTIONAL MICROPHONE — A microphone that is essentially dead to sounds arriving from either side.

BITC — Burnt-in timecode. Used with off-line editing to give a visual display of running time within the picture area.

BLACK LEVEL — A measurement of the video signal with no exposure.

BOOM — Long pole with a microphone fitted on the end.

BUZZ TRACK — Audio recording of background sounds. Also Atmos or Ambient.

CAMCORDER — Complete hand-held video recording system. Contains camera and recorder in one unit.

CAMERA CARD — Cue card for each camera listing just that camera's shots.

CAPACITOR MICROPHONE — Microphone working by detecting changes in the space between two plates. Needs a voltage to make it work.

CARDIOID MICROPHONE — Directional response pattern of a microphone where the sound is essentially gathered from the front and the sides.

CCU — Camera control unit. Remote control used by the vision engineer to control the exposure and colour output of a studio camera.

CCD — Charge coupled device. Light sensitive chip in a video camera.

CHIP CAMERA — Video camera which uses CCDs instead of tubes.

CHROMAKEY — Visual effect where areas of blue in a scene are replaced with another picture. Also colour separation overlay.

COLOUR BALANCE — An adjustment made to the camera or lighting to ensure that white is seen as white and grey as grey. Ensures that all the colours are faithfully reproduced.

COLOUR BARS — A test signal of eight colours used to adjust cameras and monitors.

COLOUR TEMPERATURE — A scale used to determine the colour quality of light. The unit used is Degrees Kelvin. 5500°K is taken as daylight, 3200°K is artificial light.

COMPONENT VIDEO — Video signal where the brightness and colour signals are kept separate.

COMPOSITE VIDEO — Video signal containing all the picture and synchronization information on one signal.

COMPRESSOR — Audio device that reduces the dynamic range of a signal to a pre-determined range.

CONTRAST — The overall balance between light and dark in a picture.

CONTROL TRACK — A track on the videotape recorder where synchronization and servo speed information is recorded. Also used to display running time.

CRAB — A camera movement where the whole camera is moved sideways.

CRANE — A camera movement where the whole camera is moved upwards.

CUT — A visual transition when one picture is instantly replaced by another.

CUTAWAY — A non-specific shot used to bridge two images that otherwise would not cut together.

DAYLIGHT — Light from natural sunlight. Has a colour temperature of 5500°K.

DECIBEL (dB) — Logarithmic measurement of sound pressure.

DEPTH OF FIELD — The distance between the closest and furthest objects within a scene that are in focus.

DIAPHRAGM — The membrane within a microphone vibrated by the sound waves.

DIFFUSER — A device used in front of a luminaire to soften the light output.

DIMMER — Piece of equipment used to alter the intensity of light output.

DOLLY — Movable platform on which cameras or microphones can be mounted.

DOWNSTREAM KEYER — Circuit in a vision mixer which allows caption superimposition without affecting the previous controls.

DYNAMIC MICROPHONE — Microphone which works on the dynamo principle, converting sound waves to electricity by the movement of a coil within a magnetic field.

DYNAMIC RANGE — The level of sound measured between the loudest and quietest usable sounds.

EDITING — Selecting and assembling the required audio and/or video pictures into the required order.

EDL — Edit decision list. A list of the actual times, type of visual transition and source that takes place between listed shots.

ELECTRET MICROPHONE — Microphone working on the capacitor principle but using static electricity instead of a DC voltage.

EQUALIZATION — Control on an audio mixer. Used to make small adjustments to the tonal quality of a sound.

FLOODLIGHT — Type of luminaire that produces a wide spread of soft light.

FOLDBACK — A system for feeding audio signals to the performers.

GALLERY — The name used for the studio control area.

GEL — A lighting accessory. Flameproof coloured sheets that can be placed in front of a luminaire to change its colour. Or a coloured sheet placed in front of a window to change the colour temperature of daylight.

GOBO — A lighting accessory. Shapes that can be fitted to focusing spotlights to change the shape of a light beam.

GREY SCALE — Test card that allows a camera to produce known output levels from black through grades of grey to white.

GRIP — Member of camera crew. Responsible for helping to move the camera.

GROUP — Facility on an audio mixer allowing several channels to come under the overall control of one fader.

GUIDE TRACK — An audio track that is in sync with the picture but not of sufficient quality to be used for reproduction. Used at the post-production stage to allow accurate replacement with good quality audio.

HARDLIGHT — A luminaire which has a housing and bulb designed to produce light with well-defined shadows.

HIGHLIGHT — The brightest part of the picture.

HYPER-CARDIOID MICROPHONE — A microphone with a very narrow response angle.

INSERT EDIT — An edit where a new picture or sound is used to replace an existing one.

JUMP CUT — A video transition where a picture cuts to a similar picture producing a jarring visual cut.

KEYER — Part of a vision mixer. Produces an effect where a hole is cut in the main picture and replaced with another picture or caption.

KEY LIGHT — The main luminaire that is used to light a performer.

LIGHTING GRID — The gantry above a studio floor from which the luminaires are suspended.

LINEAR — Term used to suggest that images are time sequential.

LONG SHOT — Camera shot which shows the whole of a person or the general view of a scene as if viewed from a distance.

LOW KEY — Lighting which has high contrast but few bright areas.

LTC — Longitudinal timecode. Timecode recorded along the length of a track.

LUMINAIRE — An artificial light source contained within a housing.

LUMINANCE — 1. Video signal containing information about the brightness of a scene. 2. The brightness reflected from a surface.

MICROPHONE — A device which converts sounds in the form of changing air pressure into electrical pressure.

MIX — 1. A visual transition where one picture is slowly replaced by another. 2. Combining of audio sounds to add, for example, voice and music on one track.

MIX DOWN — The final audio mix where all the sounds are combined.

MULTI-TRACK — An audio recorder which has more than two tracks all of which can be played back or recorded on independently.

NEUTRAL DENSITY (ND) — A filter which cuts down the light level but does not affect the colour.

NODDIES — Mute pictures of an interviewer or guest used as cutaways.

NON-LINEAR EDITING — Computer based editing system which allows editing in random order.

OFF LINE — Linear editing on low-cost equipment to produce a rough cut version and a log to be used for the final edit.

OMNIDIRECTIONAL — Directional response of a microphone where sounds are picked up from all directions around the microphone.

PAN — A camera movement where the camera is swung horizontally left or right.

PAN AND TILT HEAD — Mounting fitted between the camera and the tripod to allow vertical or horizontal movements.

PEDESTAL — Camera support with wheels and smooth vertical movements.

PHANTOM POWER — A system allowing electricity to be fed to a capacitor microphone along the audio cables.

PLUGE — Picture line-up generating equipment. Test equipment used to produce known video test signals.

POLAR DIAGRAM — Visual representation of the directional pick-up response of a microphone.

POST-PRODUCTION — The final stage of programme production where all the special effects, graphics and audio mixing are carried out.

PRE-ROLL — The time needed for a video tape recorder to go from rest to the correct speed with stable pictures.

PREVIEW — In editing, viewing an edit without it being recorded.

PROPS — Term used for all the property required by the set and performers.

RADIO MICROPHONE — Microphone which is fed to a small radio transmitter. Enables microphones to be used without cables trailing around the set.

REVERBERATION — Audio effect of recording in large spaces. Similar to echo.

RIFLE MICROPHONE — Type of microphone with a very narrow directional response angle.

RUN THROUGH — Full-speed rehearsal. Last rehearsal before recording.

SAFE AREA — Area within the frame of a picture that will be reproduced by a domestic television set.

SCENE — The minimum length of continuous action that can be recorded.

SCRIM — Lighting accessory designed to diffuse the output of a luminaire.

SHOT — A scene which is recorded as one continuous take.

SOFTLIGHT — A luminaire with its housing and bulb arranged to give a diffused, almost shadowless, light output.

STAGGER THROUGH — The first stage of rehearsal, where technical problems can be ironed out.

STORYBOARD — Pictorial representation of the programme. It should also contain the outline script and music or effects.

SYNC — Shorthand term for synchronization. Refers to sound that is in sync with the picture as in lip-sync.

TAKE — Part or all of a scene that is recorded without a break.

TALKBACK — Intercommunication system by which the director can talk to the crew.

TALLY LIGHT — Red light fitted to cameras, monitors and vision engineering panels to indicate which camera is in use.

TELECINE — A system for converting film images to video.

TELEJECTOR — A system for converting images from slides to video.

TILT — A camera movement where the whole camera is tipped vertically downwards or upwards.

TIMECODE — A digital signal recorded onto a video or audio tape to locate the exact time position in frames, seconds, minutes and hours.

TUNGSTEN LIGHTING — Artificial lighting derived from bulbs with tungsten filaments.

VECTORSCOPE — Special type of test equipment which can display the video signal in the form of amplitude or colour phase.

VITC — Vertical interval timecode. Timecode that is recorded on the picture track between each frame.

VOICE OVER — Audio recording made to support the pictures but without the performer being seen.

VOX POPS — The voice of the people. A collection of opinions or answers to questions from a representative group of the public.

WALK THROUGH — Second stage of rehearsal, carried out after the technical problems have been sorted out, to check camera angles and shots are correct.

WINDSHIELD — Cover fitted to a microphone to cut down on wind noise.

WIPE — A visual transition where one picture is replaced by another either vertically, horizontally or diagonally.

ZOOM — A camera lens movement increasing or decreasing the image size.